Russian Magic

'I highly recommend this marvellous book. The author reminds us of what too many have forgotten: that at the heart of human cultures is living nature, as manifest in local animals, places, and the land. Culture with soul arises out of an ensouled world ... Some people, of course, have never entirely lost this vital connection, and she shows how the ways of life in Russia and Siberia are ripe for rediscovery.'

— Dr Patrick Curry, University of Kent

'Through an intricately woven pattern of research and personal experience, Cherry Gilchrist draws us into the magical landscape of Mother Russia. A fascinating, informative read.'

— Virginia Rounding, author of *Catherine the Great*

'Based on extensive personal experience and research, backed up by the existing academic studies of the subject, this book offers lucid and accessible insights into a traditional culture which is, astonishingly, still flourishing in the modern world. It is packed with information about surviving folk customs, indigenous religion and traditional cosmology.'

— Prudence Jones, co-author of *A History of Pagan Europe*

Russian Magic

Living Folk Traditions of an Enchanted Landscape

Cherry Gilchrist

THEOSOPHICAL PUBLISHING HOUSE
Wheaton, Illinois * Chennai, India

First published as *The Soul of Russia* by Floris Books, Edinburgh
First Quest Edition 2009

Quest Books
Theosophical Publishing House
P. O. Box 270
Wheaton, IL 60187-0270

www.questbooks.net

Cover image: Lev Lominago, *Firebird*, www.lominago.com.
Cover design by Margarita Reyfman

Library of Congress Cataloging-in-Publication Data

Gilchrist, Cherry.
Russian magic: living folk traditions of an enchanted landscape / Cherry Gilchrist.
—1st Quest ed.
p. cm.
Rev. ed. of: The soul of Russia. Edinburgh: Floris Books, 2008.
Includes bibliographical references.
ISBN 978-0-8356-0874-9
1. Mythology, Slavic—Russia (Federation). 2. Legends—Russia (Federation). 3. Superstition—Russia (Federation). 4. Russia (Federation)—Folklore. I. Gilchrist, Cherry. Soul of Russia. II. Title.
BL940.R8G55 2009
398.0947—dc22 2009010306

4 3 2 1 * 09 10 11 12 13 14

Printed in the United States of America

Contents

Acknowledgments

I should like to thank all my amazing Russian friends who, over the years, have initiated me into Russian life and culture, plied me with vodka, led me out into the forest, and entertained me with stories and anecdotes. They have also given me interviews, written fascinating emails, lent me books and newspaper cuttings, and been very supportive of my research. These include: Vladimir and Ludmilla Fishook, Natasha and Viktor Malkov and family, Anatoli Kamorin, Pyotr and Olga Mityashin, Nikolai Baburin, Sergey Mukhin, Andrei Petrov, Masha Springford, Sergey Scheck, Ala and Alex Ilin, Nelly Fedorova and the 'Brigada' of women artists at the Kholui studio.

Special thanks go to Natalia Danilin and Vlad Shilinis in the USA, who very kindly read through the initial draft of this book and offered suggestions for corrections and additions, including stories of their own experiences from their Russian homeland.

I would like to thank my partner Robert for putting up with a writer who had her head buried deep in books while researching this project, and who went round muttering about Russian wizards and wolves, and frogs that were really princesses, whenever she came up for air. His loving support and kindness was a lifeline to me!

I would also like to thank Nick Campion and Patrick Curry of the Sophia Project, formerly at the University of Bath Spa, for encouraging me to write about Russian traditional beliefs as part of my MA course there, and for asking me to speak at the subsequent Sky and Psyche conference, which led to a fortuitous meeting with Christopher Moore of Floris Books, who I should like to thank also for inviting me to write this book and for patiently answering my queries throughout its creation. And finally, warm thanks go to my agent Doreen Montgomery, who, as always, has been a tower of strength and a source of wisdom in helping me to get the show on the road!

I owe a great debt to Russia, a country which dominated my life and haunted my dreams for over fifteen years. I wish happiness and prosperity to her people, and hope that her remarkable traditions and wonderful landscape will be preserved for the generations to come.

Introduction

I was lucky enough to visit Russia nearly sixty times between 1992 and 2006. I witnessed the transition between the Soviet era and post-communist Russia, a period of heady change, followed by the building of a new state, with all its ongoing economic and social problems. I got to know the cities of Moscow and St Petersburg well, mastered their metro systems and learnt Russian so that I could converse with reasonable fluency. But the essence of Russia for me is not so much its urban sophistication or its grand imperial legacy from the courts of the Tsars; it is the life of village and countryside, a traditional culture that has been practised unchecked through all the centuries of tumultuous Russian history. Embedded in this culture is the mythology of old Russia, its magical customs and beliefs, its relationship between human beings and nature, and its sense of the supernatural, the belief in a world not merely material but infused with spirit.

Although this culture is largely associated with rural areas, yet it influences Russians in all parts of society. Everyone in Russia spends time in the countryside, following the traditional way of life there, if only for a short period each year. Everyone knows the favourite Russian fairy stories, Russia's nature spirits and old gods, and they are a constant source of inspiration for artists, writers and composers. The Russian magical tradition sustains its people and provides a sense of heritage and continuity.

During my visits to Russia, I stayed many times in country villages. I made friends there, learnt about their hopes and beliefs, lived from time to time in a wooden village house, and experienced the rural way of life — fetching water from the well, washing clothes in the river, picking mushrooms and berries in the forest. My work at that time was to seek out its traditional arts and crafts, and exhibit them in the UK, and the art form that I came to love above all others there was the Russian lacquer miniature. These miniatures depict myths and legends, calendar customs and village scenes. I would often gaze for hours at these exquisite paintings, and they became the gateway through which I entered the world of Russian mythology, whetting my appetite to learn more about the tradition from which they had sprung. (For further details, see www.firebirdarts.co.uk.)

I also toured parts of Russia, visiting Karelia and Murmansk in the north, areas around the Volga and Nizhni Novgorod in central Russia, and took an unforgettable trip to Tuva and Khakassia in southern Siberia, where the fascinating animistic culture that survives today is akin to the cosmology that prevailed throughout Russia in ancient times. Almost everywhere I went, there was a local ethnographic or folk museum, kept with devotion and passion by its curators, and here too I learnt much about old Russian customs. This was another source of inspiration which I plumbed as best I could, often scribbling notes hastily as we spent just one or two precious hours there while I was leading one of my tour groups around, or making a research trip with colleagues. Other research was done later, from the library of books I gathered from my travels, supplemented by some excellent studies on Russian folklore published in the USA; these are all cited in the Bibliography.

I make this a personal introduction to the magic and mythology of Russia because we need to engage with it as individuals to bring it alive. The combination of field research, input from experts, and background research will, I hope, make this both an enjoyable and a sound study. It also demonstrates that Russian folklore is not just contained in erudite volumes and consigned to the past, but that it is very much a part of contemporary life in Russia, and is also intimately connected with the Russian psyche and spiritual values.

The scope of this book

My task is therefore to create a living picture of Russian myth and magic. To this end, I have not attempted to cover every detail of Russian folklore, since meaning is not always to be found in encyclopaedic detail. I have used current-day examples to set the context, as well as those from past times. This is mythology in the making, and personal experience can play a part in this. We need to take an imaginative approach to find the living spirit of the Russian tradition; we need facts and scholarly research, but these are a solid foundation for what is really a personal relationship with a mythology.

By approaching the theme in this way, I hope to offer a key to others who, like me, are intrigued by Russian culture. Perhaps you visit Russia, or have Russian relatives, or just have an inexplicable fascination with all things Russian. During my own visits to Russia, I learnt more and more about life there, but at the same time realized definitively that I am not Russian, and will never be completely a part of its culture. Inevitably, therefore, I write this from a Western standpoint, but at the same time I believe that a foreigner's view can be useful. Often those who are immersed in a culture do not consciously notice its details, or think about how to explain it, so that an outsider can sometimes shed new light on it. What I write however, is infused with a love of Russian culture, its people and its landscape. It is an interpretation, but I have taken pains to ensure that my sources are sound, and to point out what is speculative, and what is generally accepted as fact. Although most readers of this book will probably live in the West, I hope that nevertheless it may appeal to Russians who find some value in the way that a foreigner, a *chuzhoi,* dares to take a view on their culture and to celebrate its magic.

A note on gods, land and chronology

The traditions and lore described in this book are taken mainly from the last two hundred years or so of Russian culture. This forms the current body of knowledge about Russian myth and folklore which is recognized today by scholars and by the Russian people themselves, a heritage which is a part of common knowledge, even if not completely in current practice. It is almost impossible in any case to make an absolute demarcation between what is current and what is obsolete, and I treat the Russian tradition here as a river which runs through the centuries, changing almost imperceptibly as it flows. The Siberian traditions that I have drawn are to some extent separate from Russian ones today, but they are wonderful pointers to the kind of culture that once prevailed in Russia before the coming of Christianity, and they do explain the ground of what makes up the Russian tradition. However, in general, where much earlier traditions and deities are referred to, I have made it clear that these are from a bygone period. In the Epilogue, I have attempted to bring matters up to date, by introducing the new wave of Russian spirituality and neo-pagan movements, some of which seek to revive the ancient gods. But perhaps it is too early to know how they will be absorbed into this flow of Russian culture, and so in general, I have kept to that which has been passed down through oral tradition, family customs, or within everyday life.

I have avoided the word 'pagan' wherever possible, and prefer to talk about the 'native tradition' or 'traditional culture'. Although the word 'pagan' is used frequently nowadays, the dictionary definition is that of 'heathen', with origins that mean 'rustic', and this implies an earlier idolatrous or naïve belief system that was supplanted by the coming of one of the monotheistic or major religions. Although I accept that the human mind and spirit may evolve over the centuries, I do not think that earlier religions were necessarily inferior, and a renewed interest in so-called 'primitive' or indigenous belief systems today both by anthropologists and spiritual seekers, shows that they may have much to teach us.

Just as the Russian magical traditions cannot be fixed too firmly within a time frame, so the geography of what constitutes Russia is also fluid, to some extent. As a country, Russia has been through many historical changes, first expanding and now contracting again after the fall of the Soviet Empire. Its origins are obscure; the exact timing of the arrival of Slavic people into the area is still uncertain, though we know that the first kingdom of Rus, as Russia was originally called, was founded in AD 839, and was centred on Kiev, now in the Ukraine. Later, the Russian Empire expanded to the north and east, and in Soviet times also extended to cover non-Slavic areas in Central Asia and the Caucasus. During this period, ethnic Russians were also re-homed, often forcibly, in these areas and in the Baltic States, so there is no straightforward division today of Slavic and non-Slavic territory, either inside or outside post-Communist boundaries. Nor can the distinction be made on grounds of language. If you speak Russian, you will get by just as well in Samarkand as in Moscow, since Russian has become a kind of *lingua franca* in these new republics. For the purposes of this book, I have therefore made no hard and fast definition of what constitutes Russia and Russian, though in general most traditions that I focus on relate to central or European Russia. I draw on Siberian culture, and indicate where it may relate to traditional Russian culture, but acknowledge that it is a separate ethnic entity today.

No research is ever complete; I am continually finding more fascinating examples and customs in the Russian tradition, which space and time prevent me from adding to the material in this book. I hope, however, that I have created a sound framework for any further investigation that you may wish to make, and that the book will be able to lead you into the enchanted world of Russian mythology.

Cherry Gilchrist, 2009

1

The Russian Magical World

The White Stone

'This stone has been the centre of the universe for the people who live here,' Leonid explained. 'A cultural axis, a place where children are blessed with names to protect them, and illnesses are healed.'

The burly archaeologist pointed to the standing stone set in the middle of a southern Siberian plain, a solitary mountain rising behind it (see Fig. 4).

'It is called the White Stone. We know for sure that it has been used for over two thousand years, but it is much older than that. We have watched what the local people do when they visit it to make a wish, and now, if you like, you may do the same.'

Our small group, consisting of half a dozen Russians and two English women, listened intently. We were all keen to take part in Siberian good luck rituals, and had notched up one or two already, tying ribbons onto the gaunt branches of shrines to the spirit of the land.

'You must walk around it three times in a circle. As you begin, you are still in this world, but when you go round you will be led into another world. Be ready to give something as an offering — a coin or cigarette will do. Then hold the stone for about twenty seconds, women standing on the south side, men on the north. No longer, or the energy will be too strong and it could harm you.'

One of the Russian men was already moving towards the stone, eager to try the experiment.

'And you must go sunwise! Khakassians do everything this way, even when they dig their gardens.' Leonid was the chief archaeologist of the Khakassian region, and his life's work was centred on their culture, linking ancient sites with contemporary belief.

'What will happen if you go the other way?' asked Lyn, my travelling companion.

'Then you will be led into the realm of death and the ancestors,' was the simple answer.

That was enough to convince us not to tamper with Siberian traditions.

One after another, our group walked solemnly towards the stone and circled closely around it, holding the rock with both hands for the short period prescribed, after placing a small offering at its foot in exchange for the benefits that would bring us.

'Locals frequently come here,' said Leonid. 'They say the White Stone can help with cardiac disease, with kidney problems, and even to get rid of bags under the eyes! And up until the 1960s, it was a special place for children. A child who was sick could be set on the road to recovery here with the help of a shaman. The shaman placed the child facing east, with its back to the stone, and asked the spirits, "What name should I give to this child to protect it?" Usually, the new name was something ridiculous, like "Puppy" or "Frog". And in exchange, the shaman cut a lock of the child's hair, and spread it on the ground around the stone. When the child was healthy again, its original name could be restored.

'A shaman performing this ritual was in personal danger, vulnerable to the influences of any forces and spirits. But the White Stone would help to protect him. It is a temple, an open temple.'

Lyn and I took our turns at circling the stone; we made our offerings and our wishes, and dropped quietly back again to join the group, who all now seemed to be in a reflective mood.

'Fifty percent of the people who visit the stone say that it brings them some kind of help or healing,' Leonid continued. 'There may be some unusual properties of the earth at this place.'

'And has anyone tried to measure these energies?' I asked him.

'Oh yes,' he said. 'Scientific teams have visited the site three times — the first expedition came from St Petersburg in 1997, the second from Tomsk, and the third from the local capital of the region, Abakan. They think that there is a high charge of radioactive energy which emerges here from underground.'

The Russian worldview

Leonid's response to my question was typical of what I have found in Russia many times over: an open-mindedness in regard to the effectiveness of ancient rituals, to a landscape empowered with unusual forces and to a world of spirits which may interact with our own. Russian scientists may seek out a scientific explanation, as indeed they are trained to do, but they do not necessarily close the door to the view that our universe has other dimensions and energies which we are able to explore in non-scientific ways too. Our encounter with the White Stone was also an indication of a yearning in the Russian soul to return to the roots of native myth and tradition, as we witnessed our Russian co-travellers eagerly connecting to the power of the Siberian landscape and its megaliths. These survivals of a magical worldview, along with the current practices of shamanism in Siberia, are similar to the kind of culture that prevailed in central and northern Russia in earlier times, as far as archaeologists and ethnographers can tell.

Archaeologists are not alone in the Russian academic and scientific community in taking an inclusive view of the world and its mysteries. There has always been tolerance and 'perfect co-operation' between the practitioners of 'official medicine' and folk healers, for instance (Kourenoff & St George, pp.5–6). It is common for Russian hospitals to employ a psychic healer on their staff, known as an 'extra-sensor'. When Vladimir, an acquaintance of mine, was a young man on national service, he turned up at the army medical clinic feeling very ill and sorry for himself. The regular doctor was not on duty that day, and instead he found himself facing the extra-sensor, who took one look at him, and said without any examination: 'Bronchitis. You'll be better in three days.' A little disappointed at first, not having been issued with pills and prescriptions, Vladimir was then more than satisfied when the diagnosis proved completely accurate.

During my travels in Russia, I discovered a keen interest among other Russian friends and acquaintances in such topics as divination, astrology, psychic phenomena, and also in encounters with nature spirits of the landscape, who we shall meet in a later chapter. Some of these interests, such as astrology, are more recent arrivals on the scene, but they are natural contemporary additions to the national heritage of folklore, magic and mythology, which almost every Russian embraces warmly as part of his or her birthright. Perhaps the degree of openness and connection with the native tradition exists because Russian culture remained largely undisturbed for centuries. Unlike the West, the country did not experience an influx of Arabic learning in medieval times, bringing new developments in mathematics, medicine, astronomy and astrology, nor was there a comparable Renaissance or a sweeping Industrial Revolution in the eighteenth and nineteenth centuries, mechanizing age-old crafts and disparaging uneconomic, superstitious folk customs.

Great changes, of course, took place during the twentieth century, and there is no suggestion that peasant belief and folk practice is just as it was two hundred years ago. Everyone is aware that some old customs have died out, and that fairy tales may not be told with the same degree of literal belief. But the stream of tradition still flows, its source far back, perhaps, in a long lost time 'when men still spoke the language of the birds' but which continues to run its course today.[1] And indeed, Russia is a country where ethnographers can still work in the field, sending out expeditions to remote parts to research seasonal rituals, crafts of toy-making that date from prehistoric times, and magical divination practices. In the mainstream of contemporary Russian life, fairy tales are still common currency for adults and children; a stock character, Baba Yaga, the fearsome witch, is often invoked to frighten naughty toddlers into submission, and the spirits of Father Frost and Snowmaiden are called upon to preside over the New Year celebrations. Russians are not, of course, alone in honouring their folk heritage, but the Russian engagement with myth and magic appears to be more whole-hearted, open-minded, and inclusive than that of their Western counterparts.

When visiting the tiny island of Kiji in the Russian north, I once again asked a local guide about its special qualities: 'Where is the most powerful place on this island? What do people consider to be its centre?'

Without hesitation or surprise, she pointed to a low hill set back from the shoreline. 'Up there,' she said. 'Two teams of scientists have come to measure it, and both agree that there is some special cosmic energy surrounding that place.'

Other local guides on the island also told me about magical occurrences, and their meetings with spirits, stories which will be recounted later. In Russia, if one has the courage to ask, people are often willing to talk about their personal experiences of the supernatural.

Russian cosmology

The gateway to the Russian tradition is still open. But what kind of a cosmology lies at its heart? Finding the structure that it embodies can be a challenge, because the mythology has changed over the centuries, and much early material has not survived. But enough remains to give us an idea of the old Russian cosmic ordering of the universe. Recovering this also helps us to understand the framework of the traditional heritage of myth and magic, and to see how various elements of it may fit together. All the components of Russian cosmology that I am about to describe have been defined by experts in the field, though not without debate, as no one can lay claim to knowing the primary Slavic model of the universe, if indeed such a thing ever existed.

In this Slavic universe, a World Tree stands at the centre. Its branches stretch up to heaven, and its roots penetrate into the ground beneath. The Tree thus spans three worlds: the middle, human world of the earth, the celestial world above, and the underworld below. This three-tiered construction is echoed, as we shall see, in various aspects of Russian culture, from folk art to house building. Triplicity itself is a key component in Russian mythology, and there are many invocations of threes in ritual and fairy tale, especially 'the thrice-nine kingdom' which is the place where marvels and wonders occur. A three-headed Slavic god, Triglav, was once worshipped, and a ninth-century Slavic stone sculpture, known as the Zbruch idol, is thought to represent the three tiers of this cosmology, each one carved with different figures or deities.[2] Stone pillar and World Tree are often interchangeable concepts, as discussed below.

We can also imagine this three-storeyed tree represented as a sphere containing three smaller spheres. Within all these spheres, the four elements of earth, water, fire and air circulate. They are the substance of life, providing the means of growth; in relation to the tree, they represent the soil and rain, fire and wind which nurture and procreate life. In traditional Russian terms, they are seen in pairs, with earth and water representing the horizontal plane, and fire and air rising vertically upwards to the heights.

The two sides of the Tree, left and right, are reflected in the fundamental duality in the Russian model of the world. Different pairs, known as 'binary oppositions', have been distinguished as a key component of Russian myth, among them 'life and death', 'wild and tamed', and 'visible and invisible' (Haney 1999, pp.48–49). The primary polarity is described as *svoi* and *chuzhoi,* meaning the familiar and the strange, oneself and the other person, or the known and the foreign. Although a tentative number of seventeen such pairings has been proposed by certain experts, there is probably no final number to be agreed on. More to the point is the strongly-held concept of opposition itself, representing a variety of contrasting states and values that are contained within the cosmology.[3] There may well be a correspondence between the two sides of this Russian World Tree, and the distinction within the human body too, which at a very early stage of embryonic growth develops a right and a left side from a previously undifferentiated state. Cranial osteopathy is a therapy that recognizes the significance of this, and one aim of treatment is to restore the body's own natural sense of left and right, which brings back balance and harmony to the organism.[4]

The shamanic inheritance

In terms of symbols, the White Stone represents an axis of the universe in the same way that the Slavic World Tree does. Although the White Stone is venerated by local Siberian people today, rather than being a part of what we might call the ethnic Russian tradition, the two motifs of the stone and the tree are connected by the religious practice of shamanism. The people of Khakassia practise shamanism today much as they have done for hundreds, if not thousands, of years; it is considered such an unspoilt region that archaeologists study modern ritual practice in order to work out interpretations for Bronze Age pictograms, which are found scratched on rocks all around the region.[5] And, as already mentioned, Siberian ritual and shamanism do relate to the Russian inheritance of myth and magic; it is thought that this kind of shamanism was once practised all over Russia, rather than just in the remote regions of Siberia where it survives today. Although the Russian Slavic people and the Siberian tribes may be now to some extent separate, shamanism was the common culture underlying both traditions. As one recent study of Russian magic puts it:

> The kind of magic which existed among the East Slavs before the coming of Christianity was, as far as one can tell, the shamanism of the *vokhvy* [an old term for a wizard] with whom the Church and state authorities in Kiev Rus struggled for a long time, and traces of which undoubtedly survived, and still survive, in popular beliefs and practices. (Ryan 1999, p.11)

Shamans are mediators between humans and the world of spirits; they ascend to the realm of the spirits, and descend to the world of the ancestors. They usually have their own spirit guide, in the form of an eagle or bear, for instance, and when in session, enter into a trance state with the aid of drumming, chanting and invocations. A shaman is often responsible for the wellbeing of his or her community, and may undergo great personal sacrifices in order to fulfil the potential of the shamanic gift, which can bring powers to heal or prophesy, to carry news from the dead and offer a glimpse of the spirits dwelling in other realms.[6]

To understand old Slavic tradition, we can assume therefore that it had this kind of shamanic basis, at least in its early days. But in the early medieval period, as rulers formalized pantheons of Slavic deities and built grandiose temples, it seems that the shamans began to lose some of their previous importance. As the Russian nation was developed, and as Christianity spread through it from the tenth century, shamans were then ignored or rejected by the authorities. The local shaman may then have changed over time into the wizard or wise woman, who continues to perform rituals and offer healing to the villagers up until the present day.

So by looking at certain elements of the shamanic tradition as it is practised in Siberia today, we may be able to gain further insight into Russian traditional culture and cosmology. New studies of Siberian shamanism are being made all the time, and the subject is probably understood better and approached more sympathetically than at any previous period in modern history. However, we should also realize that the Siberian and Slavic traditions have diverged and developed independently over the centuries, so that they are not identical, even if they have common ground.

Modern Russians who are interested in reinstating their 'native' traditions may also draw on Siberian shamanism for inspiration, and for a stronger sense of their own roots. It was no coincidence that on the trip to Siberia, several of our fellow Russian travellers turned out to be deeply interested in healing and meditation. This may cause a new flow of shamanic practice into Russian culture, which will doubtless be frowned on by those who prefer to keep the purity of national traditions. However, in fact it is probably no different from various influxes and influences over the ages, caused by travellers, visiting foreigners, and even deliberate alterations to existing folk traditions. This idea will be explored further in the Epilogue. And, in another way, we can say that this is a perpetuation of the constant Russian impetus towards the psychic and the supernatural, part of a lineage which goes back to ancient times. Looking back down the centuries, into the early days of pre-Christian Russia, it is likely that the shamans of that time were the forefathers of later Russian sorcerers, who in turn led to today's current wonder workers, a line of descent which has gained scholarly acceptance (see Farrell 1993, p.738). Knowledge may thus have been passed down directly in Russia from shaman to magician to modern-day psychic, meaning that some of the ideas and practices still current may have very ancient origins indeed.

The World Tree

As we saw earlier, for both Russians and Siberians, the symbol of a tree at the centre of the universe is a strong feature of the cosmology. There are various versions of this; the Russian World Tree is most commonly portrayed as a mighty oak tree. According to one interpretation, it grows on top of a hill; at its summit resides the thunder god, Perun, while at its base, the serpent god Volos lives under a stone (Ivanits 1992, p.30). These two gods are at war with one another, the mighty and righteous god of the heights striking at its shadowy, chthonic counterpart. The battle between them creates thunder and lightning in the middle realm of earth, as humans experience it. It is a powerful image, and derives from the time of the first surviving descriptions of Slavic pantheon of gods as they were written in the tenth century. It is similar to the Tree of Life from Norse mythology, which was known as Yggdrasill. Although Yggdrasill is an ash tree, rather than an oak, it also has branches that reach to heaven, and roots which descend into the underworld. On its summit sits the eagle, bringer of winds, and at its root lies a serpent. The serpent and eagle are at war with each other, and a squirrel acts as a messenger between them, running up and down the trunk as it carries insults from one to another. The regions of Norse and of Slavic myth are not far apart, geographically, and in actual fact one school of thought maintains that when the Vikings arrived in Russia, they were asked to stay and help to organize unruly tribes, thus forming the nation of *Rus* in the ninth century AD. So it would not be surprising if the mythology of the two peoples shares certain features.[7]

The Tree of Life is a potent, far reaching symbol which turns up in varying forms in other traditions too. It represents 'the channel of communication between the upper world, our world, and — in some cases — the lower world'. It can signify the divine unity of heavenly and human worlds: 'offerings are made in front of and even to the sacred pole which is in some quarters addressed as if it were a representative of the Supreme Being' (Diószegi & Hoppál 1978, p.32). The Assyrians and Egyptians carved it on stone, Turkic cultures wove it into their carpets, and the Indians described it as a cosmic tree that grows in reverse, with its roots stretching up into the sky. More abstract versions are also found, such as the Kabbalistic Tree of Life, which has its origins in mystical Judaism, and is a philosophical system, used as a path towards spiritual realization. It is drawn as a glyph of connecting circles and lines, encompassing all the different levels of creation.[8]

The Kabbalistic Tree of Life may seem a long way from the mighty oak tree of the Russians, but it has something strongly in common with the shamanistic cosmic tree, which in turn has a strong relationship to the Slavic tree. The Tree of Life in both traditions, Kabbalistic and shamanistic, is also a ladder, a means to make a mystical ascent into higher realms. The Siberian shamans often use a tree for this ascent, climbing upwards in trance, and encountering the spirits of the upper region, from whom they hope to gain the precious knowledge or healing power that is required. Each individual tree used by the shamans, whether it is still growing in the ground, or a stylized version made out of wood, is a representation of the cosmic tree, which has its own myth. In vision, the shaman will see it as this. One such cosmic tree, venerated by the Shors people of Siberia, is pictured as a birch tree with nine rungs that reaches up to the clouds, where it is suspended by two silken threads to the world above. As the shaman climbs, he or she must be careful not to shake the tree, otherwise snow will fall from its topmost branches, creating a blizzard on earth.

In the Russian tradition, the early World Tree of the Slavic pantheon has come down to us in varied forms. One version is found in a story known as *The Fox Physician,* which concerns an old man who plants a cabbage in his cellar. It shoots up at such a rate that he has to cut holes through the ceilings and roof of his house to accommodate it. When it grows up to the clouds and beyond, the old man decides to climb up the stalk and see what he can find there. In this world of the sky, he finds a handmill which grinds out a pie, a cake and a pot of porridge for him. Delighted with his discoveries, the old man slides back down to earth again to tell his wife, who insists on accompanying him on his next climb. Unfortunately, she falls down to earth, and the tale ends on a gruesome note as the old man is tricked by a fox who promises to bring her back from the dead but instead eats her remains!

(Phillips & Kerrigan 1999, p.91.) Another version of this story, which is related by Elizabeth Warner in her discussion of the Russian World Tree, involves an old woman who plants an acorn in her cellar, from which a mighty oak tree grows, a close connection with the image of the Russian Tree of Life described earlier (Warner 1985, p.52). The spirit of the oak tree still plays a part in Russian folk culture; he is known as Dubynia, and he is often portrayed as a mighty and strong man who carries a club. These tales of curious peasants climbing up the World Tree, and their connection to the shamans ascending into the spirit realms, may make us think again about the nature of the popular Western story *Jack and the Beanstalk,* a favourite of Christmas pantomimes.

As well as appearing in stories, the Russian Tree of Life turns up frequently in folk art. It may be embroidered on a linen towel, painted on a distaff, or carved into a wooden chest, and can be decoded as such by experts studying the symbolism depicted there (see Chapter 2, p.26). In this form, it may have been passed down through the generations, and not consciously recognized for what it was. One artist who has been directly inspired by the Tree of Life image, however, is the Russian painter Vasily Kandinsky. Kandinsky was an ethnographer in his own right, and became fascinated by the tradition of shamanism, as well as the folk art and mythology of Russia itself. He based a number of his pictures around the shamanic journey, and in *Lyrical Oval,* which he painted in 1928; for instance, he depicted the cosmic tree along with other key shamanistic motifs. Kandinsky's tree is shown here with rainbow-coloured waters of life descending from the trunk of a heavenly birch tree decked with golden leaves. (See the reference in the groundbreaking study by Peg Weiss about the influence of shamanism on Kandinsky: Weiss 1995, p.165.)

On the shamanic World Tree, human souls may hang like leaves, waiting to be born or received back into the 'otherworld' after completing an individual life on earth. The Nanai people of Siberia believed in 'enormous heavenly trees ... which sheltered the souls multiplying in the form of birds. A woman who saw in her sleep a little bird ... flying towards her became pregnant. If a child died, its soul flew back into the tree' (Diószegi & Hoppál 1978, p.439). Among some Siberian peoples, each family would have a real tree which was held sacred, and which linked them to their ancestors, and represented the wellbeing of the current members of the family. Such a principle is also found in Russian folk art, where wooden chests or walls in the home may be painted with an image of the Tree of Life, symbolizing the 'idea of happy continuation of one's kin' (Krasunov 1996, p.13).

The Tree of Life is a core symbol in Russian culture, even if layers of time and meaning sometimes have to be peeled away to reveal its presence. It is a symbol which spans the whole time frame of the Russian tradition as we know it, and the different religions which have prevailed during that time — indigenous, Slavic and Christian:

> In heavily forested Russia, trees had both practical and mythic significance ... But the Tree of Life was a more complex symbol. The idea of life beyond human measure, renewing itself each year, and the tree's strength and towering height made it both a symbol of everlasting life and the central axis of the world, linking the lower world, the middle earth, and the sky. These were valid meanings in both pagan and Christian contexts. (Hilton 1995, p.177.)

Gods and faiths of Russia

This book is primarily about Russian traditional culture, but what do we mean by the term Russia? As a country, Russia has been through many historical changes, first expanding and now contracting after the fall of the Soviet Empire. Its borders have always included different kinds of settlers and ethnic groups. Nor are Slavic people confined to Russia, but are found in different groupings in other countries of Eastern Europe. But for the purposes of this book, I am taking as my main material the traditions and beliefs of the Slavic Russians living in Russia itself, the country as we know it today. For insight into the origins and fundamental elements of Russian magical beliefs, I turn sometimes to Siberian shamanism, as is already evident, and I also sometimes use examples of Slavic beliefs from other cultures. Boundaries have been fluid, and customs have developed over time, so it would be extremely difficult to define just one watertight category of Russian traditional belief. As one writer has expressed it:

> A single coherent model of Russian native cosmology has probably never existed. However, by studying a range of folk beliefs as they have manifested over a period of time (largely the last two hundred years, with earlier references), we can see the range of these beliefs, as well as understanding something of the influence that they had on Russian life. (Milner-Gulland 1997, p.85.)

There is no clear indication as to when Slavic people arrived in the area that we now call Russia, but the first Russian nation, known as Rus, existed by the ninth century AD. As mentioned above, by the tenth century it was well established and was centred on the city of Kiev.[9] Christianity came to Russia in about 988. Vladimir, the ruler of the time, decided that it was time that his kingdom had a new faith, and sent out his emissaries to inspect each of the great religions of the day. Legend has it that they were very impressed with Islam, but when Vladimir heard that alcohol was forbidden to Moslems, he shook his head sorrowfully and said it would never do for Russia. In Byzantium, his ambassadors were overwhelmed by the glory of the Orthodox rites there, reporting that 'on earth there is no such splendour or such beauty,' and so Orthodox Christianity was adopted as the new state religion for Russia.[10]

Over the centuries, however, Christianity only spread slowly through Russian territory, and barely reached its more remote regions. And in the areas where Christianity was accepted, it was practised alongside the older, indigenous beliefs, a state which continued almost until the present day, and which led to Russia being known as the country of *dvoeverie,* or 'two faiths'. The interplay of earlier beliefs with Christianity is clearly visible in many aspects of folk culture. Christian saints, as we shall see, are joined to Slavic nature deities, the household shrine contains a mixture of Christian and pagan images, and old calendar festivals are combined with Orthodox ceremonies. Of course, other nationalities also retain some elements of earlier beliefs in their religious practices, such as the British custom of giving chocolate eggs at Easter, for instance. But in Russia the two faiths existed side by side, accepted cheerfully by ordinary folk, even when the Church railed against them. Perhaps this is another example of Russian culture to embrace duality, and set up binary opposites, as suggested above.

The duality may also extend to the idea of Rus and Russia; although Russia (or Rossiya, as it is called in the Russian language) has long been the name for the Russian country, the old term Rus still survives. It is now taken as a metaphor, to mean the old soul of Russia; Rus stands for the people of Russia, and the Russian spirit: 'Rus ... is the essential Russia, the Russia that for better or worse lives in its people's hearts ... Many poets have written about Rus — few about Rossiya' (Milner-Gulland 1997, p.2). The word Rus may come from a Persian word meaning 'light' (as in 'shining light'), giving it a mythical cast, but there again, it may also come from Old Norse, and mean 'men who row'. Whatever the case, the love of the term Rus, and its symbolic significance to Russian people, emphasizes the strength of their cultural identity, and their willingness to embrace a spiritual dimension in a national way of life.

Shortly after Prince Vladimir I came to the throne in AD 980, and before choosing Christianity as the new state religion, he officially sanctioned a specific Slavic pantheon of deities. Gods such as Dazhbog, the god of the sun, and Stribog, god of the air, were listed among them, and wooden statues were dedicated to them in a sanctuary situated next to the royal palace in Kiev. It is not clear whether these deities existed in that form prior to this time; perhaps they were chosen from those in the existing tribal religious cults, or given new names and attributes as a way of reinforcing Vladimir's reign, and establishing national identity. For our purposes, this tenth century collection of gods is not crucial, since most are no longer a part of the folk heritage investigated here. Those that are, such as Perun and Mokosh, will be considered in their own right. Still others again may have evolved into something totally different, such as a character in a fairy tale, or a nature spirit, and we will meet these on their own terms.

Storytelling

Many of these beliefs and myths were passed down through folk stories, changing over the years as they were handed down from one generation to another. Storytelling carried its own magical traditions; stories were considered to be powerful entities in their own right, which should only be told at certain times of the day or year, such as after sunset, or during the solstice periods. To tell tales or spin riddles during lambing or calving was considered highly dangerous, and it was also necessary to take care when relating any stories that might attract spirits of the water or forest. Such spirits, if they drew near to listen, could cause chaos in the home, and give children nightmares. People feared, too, that telling stories at the wrong time might bring bad luck in general, and cause the cows to stay stubbornly out at grass, or a wolf to attack the storyteller. On the other hand, stories could bring good fortune too if related in the right context, such as during wedding celebrations (see Fig. 10).

There are different types of Russian stories; up to ten varieties are recognized by scholars, of which the most important for our purposes are the fairy tale, the animal tale, the folk narrative, and the *bylina,* or epic narrative. (A useful definition of different types of folktale is given in Haney 1999, pp.8–12.) The fairy tale is one of the most significant genre of stories for this book, as its essential ingredient is always magic, and the action involves the magical transformation of its hero and/or heroine. It is often termed the 'wonder tale' in folklore studies, as it may have no fairies in it as such. Animal tales are abundant in Russia, and are often humorous, with leading characters such as fox, hen, bear and wolf showing themselves to be cunning, wise or stupid, as the case may be. Folk narratives purport to be accounts from real life, accounts of how the teller or someone known to them had a brush with the supernatural, or an encounter with a nature spirit, for instance. We will meet the *bylini,* the medieval epic tales, in Chapter 2. There are also types of stories taken from oral tradition which are termed legends, not quite so relevant for this study, but interesting in their own right. These often have historical themes, and weave fictional events around real rulers or figures from

Russian history. Such legends are not just based on characters from the mists of time, like the story of Wise Oleg, but can centre on comparatively recent figures, such as Ivan the Terrible, Peter the Great, or even Lenin himself (see Fig. 18).[11] These must have had a strong influence on popular opinion about their rulers past and present, probably more than any official propaganda, or the conventional history of their reign.

Although many stories were passed on in the home, or at social gatherings, there were once professional storytellers too. Some of the earliest recorded storytellers are the *skomorokhi,* a *skaramokh* being a type of minstrel known to have existed in Russia before Christianity and adopted there in the tenth century. They may have been descended from the earlier, indigenous priests or shamans of the land. The *skomorokhi* wielded their own form of magical power, and it was said that the legends that they sang or recited could cast a spell upon the listener (Haney 1999, p.37). The magical nature of the *skomorokh* was, in the end, their downfall; in 1648, their profession was banned by Tsar Aleksei Mikhailovich because of its pagan associations. Many of them subsequently became itinerant tradesmen, blacksmiths and tailors, who were still known as storytellers in later centuries.

There were also bardic singers, mighty and near-mythic figures in their own right. With the *gusli,* a plucked instrument, set upon their knees, they could command the hushed attention of nobility and peasants alike, and draw them into another world, into a time when heroes walked the land, and wrestled with giants and spirits.[12] Both they and the *skomorokhi* may have sung the *bylini,* the heroic epic ballads of medieval times, which form a significant part of Russia's heritage of legends and stories, and which we explore in the next chapter.

Stories remain an important part of Russian culture, and they are still highly valued today. They are valued as stories for adults, as well as for children, and every Russian is familiar with the most popular fairy stories, such as *Vasilisa the Fair, Father Frost,* and *The Frog Princess.* These are myths which connect today's generation with the creative spirit of their tradition.

'Are tales and legends important for the well-being of Russian people?' I asked Nikolai Baburin, a master painter of the lacquer miniature tradition, who has painted many of these stories and legends on his *papier-mâché* boxes over the years. (For further details of the lacquer miniature art form, see p. 66.)

'The stories that we know from birth go on living inside us,' he told me. 'And then we, as parents, have told them to our own children. So such tales possess the wise thoughts of simple people, a wisdom woven into their stories.'

The Russian repertoire of tales does live on partly through the oral tradition, but it is fair to say that much of it was fixed at the time when nineteenth century folklorists in the field gathered huge collections and wrote them down for posterity. The most famous of these was A.N. Afanasiev (1826–71), whose collections form the basis of many Russian fairy-tale anthologies today. But they are very much a live source for artists, musicians and writers. As well as the lacquer miniature artists, painters such as V.M. Vasnetsov and Mikhail Vrubel used fairy-tale themes for their work, and composers Stravinsky and Rimsky-Korsakov wrote ballets like *Firebird* and *Snowmaiden,* based on traditional stories. The genre of literary fairy tales is highly popular too; writers like Pushkin and Yershev wove their tales around traditional motifs in verse or prose, resulting in classics such as *Ruslan and Ludmilla,* and *The Little Humpbacked Horse.* Pushkin's stories in particular lend themselves to recitation, and almost every Russian can reel off the opening lines of one of these. A Russian needlewoman who I knew taught them to her parrot, who would then recite the immortal lines back to her as she sat sewing. A Russian artist of my acquaintance, over in England for an operation, astounded and somewhat worried the nurses as he began to recite Pushkin while coming round from the anaesthetic, eyes still closed.

There are thus strong threads which connect today's Russian people to their legendary past. Although, inevitably, some of the old gods are now forgotten, and many rituals and stories have been lost over the centuries, there is still much which is current. To some extent, it doesn't matter whether this is in the form of calendar customs that are still practised as they have been for generations in a remote part of the country, or a literary fairy tale which inspires an artist to paint his or her own version of the story. The Russian sense of the mythic remains, and a disposition to take an interest in magic and the supernatural. It is a living culture that accommodates old traditions, and often renews them.

2

Mother Russia and Her Heroes

I have in my possession an old Russian towel, hand woven from linen, and embroidered in red at each end of its narrow length with various motifs. The most prominent of these is a woman wearing a triangular skirt; she is standing on the back of a horse, her arms lifted and her hands upraised to the sky (see Fig. 30). It is a ceremonial towel, not for ordinary washing and drying, but used in hospitality rituals or to enfold sacred household objects. This woman is the Mother Goddess of Russia, whose depiction goes back to ancient times, and who is still found embroidered in a similar way on thousands of cloths, towels and costumes all over Russia and Slavic countries.

Her distinctive form is known to practically every Russian, but not always recognized for who she is. A Christian upbringing for some, and a rather bland, Soviet education in native folklore for others, may have concealed her true nature from general view. I once showed my antique towel, a find from a Moscow flea market, to a Russian woman of my acquaintance, and was talking excitedly to her about the embroidery of the mother goddess on it.

'Oh,' she said, with a singular lack of interest, 'We were always told that this was just the figure of a housewife.'

But experts in folklore and culture know different. Textile specialist Sheila Paine travelled extensively in remote areas to try and track down the roots of this female figure, who is found not only in Russia and Eastern Europe, but also in Central Asia and the Himalayas, where she may appear in the form of an amulet as well as in embroideries and paintings. As with the motif on the Russian towel, she is frequently shown in stylized triangular shape, her hands held up high in the 'orante' gesture of prayer or blessing.

The Russian deity is thus part of a much more widespread mother goddess cult, but she has her own identity and attributions, which are themselves broad and inclusive. A flood of ideas pours from her image. As one writer puts it: '[She] ... combines all the archaic forms of female divinity ... She symbolizes the creative forces that move all nature into activity' (Hubbs 1988, p.27). She is the body from which the Tree of Life grows and flowers; for example, a creation story from the Yakuts of Siberia describes how, when the Tree of Life rises from the golden navel of the earth, a woman emerges from the trunk of the tree, and suckles it, to aid its growth (Drury 1989, p.24). The mother goddess represents the earth, yet she is also the link with the sky, and is often portrayed with birds, sun symbols and horses, which are the sky spirits in Russian mythology (as will be explored in Chapter 4). Her shape is sometimes graceful and feminine, sometimes geometric, 'abstracted into meanders, lozenges, squares, and circles'.[1]

She may even appear in a comparatively modern version, dressed as a stylish nineteenth century lady carrying a parasol. Alison Hilton, writing on Russian folk art, discovers her thus on a painted wooden distaff:

> The composition is ... ritualistic; the key elements of bird, tree, and flanking horsemen and frontally placed female figure correspond to those in other scenes of worship before a nature goddess. The woman with the parasol, standing beneath an arch like a rainbow, suggests the rain and fertility associated on a very deep level with Mokosh, or Mother Moist Earth. The tree, the Tree of Life, links her to the upper, active zone of the sky and sun, identified with the hovering bird. (Hilton 1995, p.178.)

Mokosh and Damp Mother Earth

It is not always easy to define a specific and primary mother goddess, and it can be too tempting to label any ancient female deity as 'the great goddess'.[2] But folklorists and scholars all seem to be in accord in recognizing this Russian mother goddess, and in identifying her presence in a range of contexts, from embroideries and folk art, to various peasant traditions. Although her general origins and evolution are still cloudy, in her Russian incarnation she is identified as one of the original female Slavic goddesses; her names vary, but her existence as a powerful goddess figure goes back to pre-history, and continues right up until the present day.

In the early days of Rus, she was known as Mokosh, and her presence was officially confirmed in the pantheon of gods that was sanctioned by Vladimir I in the tenth century AD. The word Mokosh may be connected with the Russian word *mokri*, meaning 'wet', which may connect too with her other best-known name, that of *Mat' sira zemlya*, or 'Mother Damp Earth' (or 'Damp Mother Earth', as it is often more naturally translated). Whatever name she goes under, this goddess is closely bound up with the earth. Not only does she represent its fertility, but she also stands for the sacredness of the earth itself, and its identity as the earth of Russia. Thus she is Mother Russia to the Russian people as well.

The Russians are a people with a strong love for their country. If one asks a Russian, 'Why do you think, feel, or behave this way?' the answer is often, 'Because I am *Russian*.' This means to go about things wholeheartedly, to feel deep emotion, to enjoy whatever food and drink is provided, and to spend time in the countryside, acknowledging the power that the land holds over you. To be Russian is to share in the Russian soul, the *dusha*. This might mean drinking late into the night with your friends, confiding your troubles and mixing tears and laughter, or reciting Pushkin's poems at a solemn family occasion, or being drawn out to the forest, abandoning all other commitments, to pick mushrooms on a warm August morning. Even Russians who emigrate usually take with them a fondness for their native land, and a deep attachment to their heritage; in my gallery in Bath, I was once asked to pick out a Russian landscape painting for a homesick Russian bride, but I fear that the English husband who wanted to console her with this well-meaning gesture may have created just the opposite effect!

As Mokosh, the mother goddess eventually declined into a minor household deity in the north of Russia, who even in the twentieth century was renowned for punishing women who broke any ritual rules connected with spinning. Although Mokosh was no longer so prominent, nevertheless spinning has always played a key role in Russian culture, and has associations with magic, and with fate, spinning the threads of life and death.

As *Mat' sira zemlya,* Damp Mother Earth, the goddess remained fully empowered, almost until the present day. As one study says: 'Belief in the absolute sanctity of "Mother Damp Earth" ... has been central to folk belief throughout the centuries' (Ivanits 1992, p.15). People would take a solemn oath by swallowing a mouthful of earth, and in times of trouble, it was the custom to protect villages by ploughing a furrow around them, in order to open up the earth and release her life-sustaining forces. The feminine nature of this ritual was emphasized; in the time of plague, it might be carried out by a procession of women, consisting of nine maidens and three widows.

> They would all undress to their shifts. The maidens let down their hair, and the widows covered their heads with white shawls.
>
> They seized ploughs, the maidens armed themselves with scythes, and others would grab various objects of terrifying appearance, such as skulls of animals.
>
> The procession would then march around the village howling and shrieking, while they ploughed a furrow to permit the powerful spirits of the earth to emerge and to annihilate the germs of evil. Any man who had the bad luck to meet the procession was felled without mercy. (*New Larousse,* p.287.)

Damp Mother Earth was considered sacred by the Russian people, and as such she could grant absolution, even to Orthodox Christian believers. If a priest was not available, the earth would be called upon. Confessions were made to her, and even into the twentieth century, it was the practice in the Vladimir region to ask the earth's forgiveness just before one's death. For specific ceremonies too, invocations were often made to *Mat' sira zemlya;* this might involve sanctifying a space by marking each of the four cardinal points with a prayer to Mother Earth. Sometimes these might be a plea for favourable weather and harvests, such as: 'Mother Earth, calm the North winds and clouds, Mother Earth, subdue the snowstorms and the cold'.

A more poignant type of confession was made by the young bride, who used the earth as a confidante. Her married life could mean great loneliness, starting as a new and lowly member of her husband's family, relegated at first to humble tasks such as sweeping the floor and fetching water. Keeping her former girl-friends was discouraged, in case they caused trouble by spreading gossip. At her wedding, the bride was advised in a traditional song:

When you are melancholy [and] sad,
Go to a virgin field,
Fall down and pour out your soul to a hot stone.
The hot stone will not gossip,
The damp mother earth will not tell. (Worobec 1991, p.165.)

In a happier vein, respect for the earth was shown when finding and picking plants, and she would be thanked for her bounty. Herb gatherers especially were recommended to bow to the earth six times at home before setting out, then six times over the place where the herbs were found growing. Herbs have long been an essential part of folk medicine, and luck would be needed in seeking them, and gratitude when picking them. A householder's herbal advised that the following prayer should be recited three times when culling herbs for healing:

> Lord bless me. And you Mother Fresh Earth bless me to cull this plant. You have brought it forth for man's use and thus I take you. From the earth a plant, from God a medicine. Amen. (See Ryan 1999, pp. 48, 271.)

Here, once again the *dvoeverie*, or two faiths, can clearly be seen at work, in the duality of the earth mother and the Christian God (see Chapter 1, p.19). Respect and acknowledgment is given to each, and both are called upon gracefully and gratefully, without any apparent conflict of belief.

Nature

The Russians' love of their motherland is therefore strongly bound up with the age-old reverence for Mother Earth, in her Russian form. It may well be that the Russian attitude to nature is similarly influenced; there is no standard global view of 'nature' itself, which is a concept that is viewed in various ways in different cultures. In the English language, for instance, the word 'nature' seems to carry certain meanings in the way it is used; phrases such as 'leave it to nature,' 'in tune with nature', and 'the natural world' all suggest a belief in a particular kind of energy, and indeed a living spirit, which has its own volition and which will act in its own time. 'Nature' is perhaps as close as we get in modern Western society to a personified deity that is not of the Christian religion, though it is true that the old goddess Fortuna still looms large (especially in lotteries) and one might argue that Father Christmas is alive and well. At any rate, the Western sense of nature appears to be somewhat different to the Russian one. If we go straight to the Russian word for nature, *priroda,* it does not have the same active force that we associate with nature; as far as I can ascertain, *priroda* seems rather to denote landscape, pretty countryside, and panoramic views of forests and grasslands.

But the concept of Damp Mother Earth, *Mat' sira zemlya,* does carry the sense of primal being, of vegetative force and a spiritual essence of the earth, to a degree even greater than does our 'nature'. She is the primary form who embodies the natural forces in the Russian worldview. And she may also be, oddly enough, the reason for an apparent Russian disrespect for nature. On a local level, I have witnessed on many occasions how country-dwelling Russians, who genuinely love their landscape, throw away their litter into the bushes after a picnic, and don't think twice about leaving (empty) glass vodka and beer bottles stacked around the base of a tree. On a national level, there is an appalling record of pollution, even in the wildernesses of Siberia, and grandiose and disastrous Soviet enterprises were undertaken in previous decades to build dams and irrigate land at the expense of the eco-system. A new awareness of conservation is of course stirring in Russia, but there has certainly been a tendency to squander resources with no care or thought for the consequences. Could this be because Damp Mother Earth forgives all, receives all, and renews all?

When Russian villages are no longer inhabited, they are allowed to die away into the forest; when houses are abandoned, perhaps when their occupants emigrate to the city to seek work, the wooden structures simply decay and are absorbed back into their surroundings. As one writer puts it:

> There is something ineffably moving in the prospect of the traditional Russian village...formed almost entirely out of the forest all around it, ready (since wood is so transitory) to return to the forest as soon as humans no longer maintain it.' (Milner-Gulland, p.30.)

Damp Mother Earth, the closest concept to 'nature', is considered to be generous, offering an inexhaustible bounty, her fertility perpetually renewing itself. She will deal with the debris of human life, receive it back into her body and produce new growth from it. Perhaps, then, in these times of acute environmental stress, this ancient archetype, the old image of Mother Goddess, Mokosh and *Mat' sira zemlya,* needs to be consulted anew, in order to preserve her domain. Myth must develop and be re-envisioned as human society evolves, and the vulnerability of Mother Earth needs to be recognized, as well as her strength and generosity. Whereas absorbing the old timbers of homesteads is still viable, dealing with the plastics and chemicals of modern production is another matter altogether. Russians have long trusted in the resources of forests, rivers and meadowlands, not to mention oil and gas in modern times, but although the territory is huge, and rich in all kinds of natural resources, these are not inexhaustible.

Saint Paraskeva and Mother Goddess

Although the original goddess of the earth has maintained her presence in folk culture, she appears in other variants too, most notably as St Paraskeva-Friday. The Russian 'two faiths' belief system has produced some delightful combinations of Slavic deities and Christian saints, and in this case Mokosh and *Mat' sira zemlya* have shifted into the evolutionary niche offered by the cult of St Paraskeva. St Paraskeva was a virgin-martyr who lived in the third century AD, during the reign of Diocletian; her name means 'Friday' in Greek, and in Slavic culture she became known as a protectress of women and their work. Her feast day is held on October 28, a time of year that is traditionally associated with marriages, and spinning, which St Paraskeva had some jurisdiction over. At this time, young women traditionally presented towels embroidered with the image of the mother goddess, similar to the one described above, to the icon of St Paraskeva-Friday. Although St Paraskeva may be well-disposed towards women, they will suffer her annoyance if they do not honour her in the appropriate way. Just as Mokosh, the spinning deity, punished badly behaved women, so 'Mother Friday' also punishes women who do not celebrate her festivals. One woman was allegedly changed into a frog, and others were afflicted with eye disease, preventing them from any more spinning and sewing.[3]

Perhaps the most radical and significant evolution of the Slavic mother goddess was into Mary, Mother of God, as the Virgin Mary is known in Orthodox Christianity. The *orante* stance of the goddess, with hands uplifted to heaven, must have facilitated the change. Both Mary and Mokosh are associated with protection, with fertility and birth, so it may have been a natural step for Russians to accept Mary as the new, supreme female figure in a religious pantheon, even while still keeping the image of the old goddess in one form or another (see Hilton 1995, p.142).

Matrioshka dolls

From the Mother of God to Russian dolls: the famous painted wooden dolls, nesting one inside another, may well be a current form of the goddess Mokosh. These dolls are often thought of as a symbol of Russia itself, and are given the name Matrioshka, which means 'Little Mother'.[4] Matrioshka dolls are usually painted as country peasant women, commonly in sets of three, five, seven, or ten. Other designs, depicting anything from cats to Russian presidents, are often painted today, but the typical, traditional Matrioshka is a rosy-cheeked peasant lady, wearing a headscarf and an apron.

These dolls look rather simple, and you might dismiss them as a lowly craft form, so commonplace that they are not worth consideration in a serious study of Russian mythology and culture. For the visitor to Russia, the ranked armies of Matrioshka dolls, with their staring eyes and garish colours adorning every craft stall and souvenir shop, can seem more like a nightmare than a display of folk art. But if you look more closely, ignoring the crudely painted versions, made in a hurry for tourists, and focus instead on those that are simply but effectively painted, then you will notice that these have a consistency of style, creating a genuine identity for the Matrioshka doll. She has a certain kind of presence, and her clothes and decoration have their own symbolism. Artists, workshop directors and toy historians all take her seriously. In the Semyonov workshop, near Nizhni Novgorod, teams of women artists work with dedication, each of them painting one aspect of the doll. According to the director there, each feature has its own requirements and meaning. The Matrioshka's eyes must be kind; her headscarf represents protection, and her apron stands for the home. She is often painted holding a hen, the bird being an ancient Russian symbol for happiness, and her dress is scattered with flowers, which imply abundance (see Fig. 24). All her colours are those of nature: 'Her red, yellow, blue and green garments suggest the colors of blood, sunlight, ripe wheat, sky, water ...'(Hubbs 1988, p.xii).

Thus the humble nesting doll, often costing only a few pounds or dollars, is more than she seems. She can be 'everywoman', and the first goddess of the Tree of Life; she can be a modern day representation of the fundamental earth goddess of Russia. As the alchemists say, you may look for the seeds of your gold among the humble dross of everyday life; you will find it in something which is everywhere, yet overlooked by everyone (see Gilchrist 2007, p.48). Matrioshka, the little mother, is perhaps also a symbol for the family line, and the continuity of generations; sometimes the smaller dolls in the set are depicted as children, both boys and girls. In the Russian arts gallery that I ran, we sold many sets of plain 'blank' dolls, skilfully turned from lime or aspen wood.

They were extraordinarily appealing in their naked simplicity, and people loved to paint them with their own designs. Often, they planned to portray the individual members of their family on them. Sometimes whole consignments were purchased for self-development workshops, where participants used them to explore their family relationships, or took the sequence of dolls to represent different layers of their own being.

Matrioshka dolls may also be linked to the ancient goddess by way of an image known as 'Golden Woman'. This was said to be a statue of woman, probably made of gold, who contained three figures inside her body, one within the other. It was reported several centuries ago that worshippers hung golden offerings to her on a nearby tree. Whether this was pure legend is not known; however, treasure seekers from abroad marked up their maps with her possible whereabouts, and set out on expeditions to find her. One story has it that she was eventually taken away and hidden for safekeeping, so that her sacred image could never be violated. The story of the Golden Woman bears a close resemblance to the figure of the Matrioshka doll, and may also relate to a goddess from the Urals region known as Jumala, whose body contained all created things within it.[5]

So it seems that there is very little problem in identifying Russian nesting dolls with a mighty goddess figure from ancient Russia. But there is one snag: the dolls were only invented in the nineteenth century. Research indicates, moreover, that they probably came from Japan. It is thought that a Russian monk, who was living in Japan at the time, got the idea from a little set of nesting figures that he came across, and passed it on to some high-minded artists in the Moscow region, who then used it to create a new type of craft form for Russia. A children's illustrator, Sergei Malyutin, is credited with making the first documented Matrioshka in Russia in 1890. Moreover, the outer figure in the original Japanese set was not a woman, but a bald-headed old man with a beard, who represented the Buddhist sage Fukuruma. Early samples of Matrioshka dolls in Russia did not always show women either on their chief outer doll, but might depict male figures from tradition and folktales, such as 'Boyarin' (wealthy merchant), 'Grandfather Turnip', and more simply, 'Old Man'.

What are we to make of all this? If there is no direct historical link between today's nesting doll and the mother goddess, do we have a right to claim that the Matrioshka is a contemporary representation of her form? I suggest that we do; if a myth has enough power and relevance to the people of the land, it can resurface and take new forms, even if there is no literal, unbroken lineage to follow. We have already seen that the image of the goddess was retained in embroideries, that the sacredness of Mother Earth remained a feature of folk heritage, and that 'Mother Russia' is a key concept. It is also evident, looking at the brief recent history of the Matrioshka doll, that it evolved quickly and perhaps inevitably into the classic peasant woman representation. The tradition of the mother goddess was strong enough to take over the craft form, and mould it into the archetypal image that it bears today, even in a humble form. One study of the Matrioshka doll, translated from the Russian, puts it in this beguiling way:

> Even now matrioshka is considered to be a symbol of motherhood and fertility. A mother doll with numerous dolls-children perfectly expresses the oldest symbol of human culture. (Soloviova 1997, p.12.)

Male and female; ours and yours

Male and female represent a polarity, a fundamental binary opposition, and it has already been shown in Chapter 1 that this type of polarity is strong and central to Russian culture and mythology. It came into play at our visit to the White Stone, where the local ritual decreed that women should hold the stone on the south side, and men on the north. If the primary female principle in Russia is Mother Damp Earth, who or what represents the masculine force in relation to her? Possibly at certain periods in history, she might have been matched against the most powerful native male deity; the defunct deity known as Rod, god of creation and light, and the associated god of thunder Perun, have been suggested as candidates for this role.[6] But in Russian mythology as it is known and remembered today, the strongest masculine role is played by the *bogatyrs*, the heroes of old Russia. These are in some sense the mythic ancestors of today's Russia, creating and defending her in centuries gone by.

Mother Earth and the *bogatyrs* thus form one kind of polarity, as male and female energies that shape the nation. But combined together, they represent one end of another axis, a key binary opposition identified by folklorists as 'oneself and the other', or 'us and the foreigners'. *Bogatyrs* defended the sacred earth against invaders, and even in more recent, less legendary times, Russia has been a heavily guarded country. The myth of Damp Mother Earth has both strengthened the Russian sense of identity, and encouraged a suspicion of foreigners and anything *chuhzoi,* which means foreign, strange, or 'other'. Even today, although individual friendships between foreigners and Russians may blossom, the prevailing official culture remains one of keeping Russian borders tightly sealed, and restricting movements of foreigners within the country. The overall sense of 'us and them' remains a powerful force in modern times, and the rules governing visas and travelling around the country now are almost as strict for visitors as they were during the Communist era.

Laurens van der Post drew attention to this phenomenon, the sense of 'us' and 'ours', when he visited Soviet Russia in the 1960s, and witnessed one of the gigantic May Day parades held in Moscow at that time. As some fifty thousand men marched onto Red Square, van der Post listened to what his fellow Russian spectators were saying:

> Now for the first time I heard a word used which has great meaning and power in Russia. Someone near me speaking of the soldiers, breathed with deep satisfaction the word *'nash'* (that is, 'ours'). (Van der Post, p.199.)

Bogatyrs: *the Superheroes*

At a party in a Moscow flat, I asked a young Russian what the true meaning of the word *bogatyr* was. I kept coming across it in stories, but couldn't work out exactly how it fitted into the traditional scheme of heroes and heroines. We were just celebrating the end of a seminar comparing Russian and Celtic mythology, so I knew he would be well in tune with the subject. He thought for a moment, and then replied, 'It is a hero with the force of nature behind him.'

This answer satisfied me then as it does now. A *bogatyr* is more than a conventional hero; he is, metaphorically at least, a giant hero, someone who strides through the land of Rus. He undertakes mighty deeds, wins impossible battles, and honours his mother country. Our conversation was in English, but as he was a native Russian speaker, his use of the word 'nature' could have referred either to Damp Mother Earth, or the Western idea of the force of nature — both are possible, for what comes across is the sense of a hero who is larger than life, and empowered by the elements. He acts in accord with the spirit of the land, and his deeds thus have lasting impact.

The *bogatyrs* are found chiefly in the *bylini,* the epics of early Russia mentioned in the previous chapter. No one knows, in fact, exactly how early they are. Many of them seem to date from the tenth to the fourteenth centuries AD, from the time of Rus and the Kievan period, as it is known, onwards. However, some have more ancient origins, such as the *bylina* of the hero Volkh Vseslavyevich whose adventures bears the mark of earlier, shamanic magical practices.[7]

The word *bylina* itself (plural *bylini)* is, rather disappointingly, a comparatively modern term, introduced only in the 1830s. Its meaning is connected with the verb 'to be', and signifies 'something that was'. *Bylini* were collected from oral tradition in the nineteenth and early twentieth centuries, largely in the far north of Russia; one of the first recorders was P.N. Rybnikov; in 1860 he was driven to find shelter when caught in a storm while travelling on Lake Onega. He found himself on a small island, where various other travellers had also taken refuge, and were keeping each other amused with stories and singing. As he lay in a pleasant doze, following his storm-tossed ordeal, he was aroused by the 'strange sounds' of a *bylina* being sung, the first he had ever heard. 'Lively, whimsical, and cheerful, it at times became faster, at times broke off, and recalled something ancient that people of our time had forgotten' (Bailey & Ivanova 1999, p.xv). Rybnikov, now excited and fully alert, lost no time in noting down the songs, which he recognized as embodying various ancient stories that were thought to have died out in the oral tradition. From that moment on, he became a devoted collector of the *bylini,* and others followed in his footsteps.

The *bylini* were generally sung, with a melody, or as a kind of semi-sung, semi-spoken narrative, similar to the way in which recitative is performed in opera and oratorio. In fact, recitative itself is thought to have derived from bardic performers who wandered from town to town in Italy in medieval and Renaissance times, often chanting or singing to a resonant chordal accompaniment given by a stringed instrument. Performers of Russian *bylini* sometimes used a *gusli,* or perhaps sometimes sang without any instrument. (For a definition of *gusli,* see Chapter 1, note 12.) Some were the medieval equivalent of the troubadours, the *skomorokhi* whom we met in Chapter 1, and others may have been dedicated bards, singers of epic poetry. There were female singers of *bylini,* too, especially in the latter years when the tradition had passed into the general population.

The *bylini* may vary from a length of about three hundred lines up to a thousand; in the field of epic poetry, this is relatively short, since epics longer than the Bible have been recorded in Central Asia! Although *bylini* became the possession of peasant audiences and singers, originally they were sung to nobility and royalty, and composed with them in mind. As already mentioned, folklorists began to collect what they could, before it was too late, and recorded hundreds of versions which have since been collated and studied. Now there are no more native singers of *bylini,* but the tradition has gained a permanent place in Russian heritage, and the poems of the *bylini* have come back into popular culture.

Bogatyrs are the principal characters of the *bylini.* They are superheroes, often growing at an unnatural rate from birth, and possessing superhuman strength. One infant *bogatyr* 'didn't grow by the year, but by the hour', for instance (Bailey & Ivanova 1999, p.40). Another young hero was so strong that 'his jokes were no laughing matter'; if he grabbed someone's arm in a merry manner, the arm was usually wrenched off. Once grown, and in command of their powers, *bogatyrs* move into action. The *bogatyr* is usually dressed in special armour, and mounted on a noble horse that is decked out with a finely made saddle, with a splendid saddlecloth, and perhaps silken girths and golden buckles. Thus armed and caparisoned, he will fight off any invaders who threaten the kingdom of Rus. Dragons are also worthy foes; *bogatyr* Dobrinya Nikitich, mounted on his noble horse, has to trample over a whole thicket of baby dragons in order to challenge the chief dragon, and rescue the maiden it holds prisoner in a cave. Sometimes clumsy and ignorant to start with, the *bogatyr* develops rapidly in his role as warrior, hero and protector. Much is achieved through his great strength and stature, but in some of the *bylini* the *bogatyrs* also have magical powers; the ancient hero Volkh Vseslavyevich, his name meaning 'Wizard of the Slavs', learns magical skills rather than fighting techniques, for instance. The 'first wisdom' he acquires is to turn himself into a bright falcon, the second into a grey wolf, and the third into an auroch with golden horns.

A *bogatyr* also gathers around himself a *druzhina,* a band of men, who will support him and fight for his causes. He may fall in love with a princess, and fight for her sake, or woo her in some other way. There are indeed some women *bogatyrs,* the female version being known as a *bogatyrka,* among them Nastasia, daughter of the king of Lithuania, who is 'always roaming and looking for a fight'. Her downfall lies in her skill in shooting arrows; when she beats the hero Dunai in an archery contest, he kills her in anger. The warrior maiden does play a strong part in certain *bylini,* and has come down to us in certain fairy tales, such as *Maria Morevna,* the story of a princess who, although war-mongering, is also wise and loving, and helps to save her husband from various dangerous enchantments.

It is the male hero who is most prominent, however, in the *bylini,* representing an upsurge of strong masculine energy and action in adventures that take place during the early days of the Russian nation. In fact, although there is some scope for dating the approximate origin of the legends, the Russia of the *bogatyrs* is in one sense timeless. These are the stories of a land through which heroes ride, the mythical Russia of danger and action, of deeds and characters larger than life. The *bylini* epitomize the noble spirit of Russia, and are pervaded by a heady mix of heroism and magic. They set the scene for a Russia that arouses a sense of awe in her people, and whose mythic roots can be venerated for all time.

The connection with Mother Earth is made plain, as *Mat' sira zemlya* is mentioned and invoked in many of these *bylini,* and she is acknowledged as the ground from which these heroes spring. The *bogatyr's* mother may also be a personification of *Mat' sira zemlya.* She is typically described as an honourable widow (and so a primary and lone female parent, in accord with the archetype) who is devoted to her son, and who acts as a source of wisdom to the young *bogatyr.* She sees his potential, encourages his education, and warns him away from danger, advice which he may or may not take. Where a father is indicated, he may also relate to the earth. In the ancient epic of Volkh Vseslavyevich, the hero's mother, a princess, is impregnated by a serpent, which in itself represents a chthonic underworld deity, associated with the dark recesses of the earth. The child that is born to her demands strong steel armour when he is only an hour and a half old, but his mother manages to temper his impetuousness, by making him learn to read and write.

Another of the oldest epics concerns Svyatagor, a primordial hero whose strength during his day makes him the mightiest power in the land. But when his reign is over, he gives himself back to Damp Mother Earth. Svyatagor is a wise, solitary and unique character, more of a deity on earth than a superhuman hero. As with all the prominent epic heroes of the *bylini, h*is legend has found a permanent place in Russian hearts. His was the first image that I acquired on a Russian lacquer miniature in St Petersburg, at the start of my travels in Russia in 1992. (For further details on lacquer miniature painting, see p.66). As I wrote at the time:

'I held the little box in my hands. It was the first lacquer miniature that I had bought, and I was terrified that I had made the wrong choice. It glowed with colour; on it a spirited horse was painted in flame red, ridden by an armed knight whose spangled cloak blew upwards in a swirl of orange and gold. The knight was gazing up at a huge figure towering above him: Svyatagor, a giant warrior mounted on an earth brown steed, caparisoned in green and gold.

Above them both, clouds curled in stormy clusters, their shading subtly reflecting the greens and oranges of the rocky foreground. This was the scene on the lid of the box, which I now opened, revealing the warm red lacquering inside.

I was reassured. The vigour and movement in the painting, and the drama of the encounter between the two knights, spoke to me of a real artist at work, someone who had engaged with the spirit of the legend. More than that, it seemed to draw me into the heart of a Russia that I was searching for, but could scarcely find in the grimy grandeur of urban St Petersburg. As yet, I knew practically nothing of the lacquer miniatures as an art form, but I could see in this box the essence of Russia. It gave me a sense of the mythic heritage whose influence has shaped the fortunes and culture of the Russian people over hundreds if not thousands of years.'[8]

The story of Svyatagor is one of 'a change of generations among epic heroes' (Bailey & Ivanova 1999, p.13). Svyatagor was once the ancient guardian of the land, but he is finally challenged by the famous *bogatyr* Ilya Moromets, hero of a new Russia, of Kievan Rus, with its sophisticated knights who are full of bravado. Svyatagor's downfall begins when he is out riding one day, and finds a tiny *skoromokh's* bag. But although it looks a mere trifle, he finds that he cannot lift it from the ground, even when he uses all his strength. It drags him down into Damp Mother Earth herself, but the first time that this happens, he is saved by his horse who pulls him out again. Then he encounters Ilya Moromets; it is nothing to him to start with to brush off the young upstart *bogatyr,* and they even make a pledge of friendship, but at last Ilya Moromets gains supremacy when Svyatagor lies down in a coffin to test out its size, and finds he cannot get out again. Svyatagor recognizes that his time is over, and asks his successor to bury him 'in the damp earth' a force that he can no longer resist, and to which he must now return. As a parting gift, he breathes on Ilya's 'white face' to give supernatural strength to the young hero.

Bogatyrs, a seemingly similar posse of daring young heroes, are actually differentiated and characterized to a significant degree. They are individual creations springing up from the mother soil of Russia, proud of their different skills and achievements. The three best known *bogatyrs,* who are often grouped together, are Ilya Moromets, Dobrinya Nikitich and Alyosha Popovich, and they each have their own characters and tasks. Alyosha is something of a trickster, Dobrinya is famous as a dragon-slayer, and Ilya as a defender of the Kievan state. Other different *bogatyrs* include Sadko, a skilful merchant and a singer whose performances charm even the King of the Waters. The *bogatyr* Churila Plyonkovich is also a case apart, a dandy and a ladies' man, who 'shakes his yellow curls' and 'jingles his gilded rings' to win the women's attention at court. He is known for making trouble, being quick to take advantage of a husband's absence to slip into bed with a favoured lady.

In the theme of Mother Russia and her heroes, we therefore have something of the archetypal distinction of the feminine and masculine forces that underpin Russian culture. Damp Mother Earth gives birth to her sons, and receives them back again when their time is over. The heroes are educated by their mothers, whether their birth mother or the land itself, but individuate themselves, striving to reach their full potential of strength, prowess and cunning. Both Mother Earth and the *bogatyrs* have a place in the Russian cultural heritage as it is expressed today, and the two types of beings may, when taken as a fundamental polarity, help to shed light on aspects of traditional Russian culture. There is food here, too, for relating the psychology of Russian gender studies to Russian mythology, but my concern here is with the myth itself, and I leave those explorations to others in the field.[9]

3

The Russian House and the Craft of Living

A visitor travelling through the Russian countryside soon learns to pick out the typical Russian village house. It is made of wood, usually of logs, but sometimes of planks, and often cheerfully painted in colours such as ochre, sea green, light blue or burnt umber. It clusters with its neighbours for community, but is set comfortably in its own plot, with a spacious vegetable garden at the rear, and perhaps a small strip planted with flowers at the front. Ramshackle wooden barns and storehouses are tacked onto what may appear to be a single storey dwelling, though often a little dormer window may give a hint of a room upstairs. The house is decorated with carved lacy fretwork around the windows, and frequently the ornamental carving is extended to face boards, gables, porches and balconies. Although the style and size of the houses vary from region to region, the observant newcomer will detect the underlying blueprint that constitutes the traditional Russian home.

House as microcosm

The Russian house is more than a practical home for day-to-day living; it is a model of the universe, a microcosm in its own right. Although the house may look at first sight as though it only has a ground floor, closer investigation usually reveals a trapdoor in the floor of the living quarters leading to an underground cellar, and very often an unheated attic room above. The way it is built embodies the three levels of creation, so that just as there are three vertical worlds represented in the Russian Tree of Life, each house also has its underworld, a human or middle world, and an upper world connecting it to the sky.

> The house, where many generations of a peasant family lived and died, was associated by its inhabitants with a small universe, connected innately with the world of nature and the Cosmos. Peace and harmony should be reigning in this well-ordered world — once and forever. (Krasunov 1996, p.12.)

Everything in the traditional Russian house is charged with meaning. It is considered to be an entity in its own right, a vital living space which must be laid out according to the rules of the cosmos, and in which certain rites should be carefully observed to keep it in good health as a home, and beneficial for the humans who live there. If you visit an ethnographic or outdoor buildings museum in Russia (of which there are many), you are likely to be bombarded with information on this theme.

'The first person to go into the newly built house would also be the first person to die!' announced our guide enthusiastically, as my tour group stood at the entrance to a historic wooden house in the outdoor museum at Suzdal. 'So who do you think they sent in first?'

'The grandfather?' someone piped up.

'No!'

'The mother-in-law?' tried another person.

'No. The cat!' she concluded triumphantly, to general laughter, as she had plainly done many times before.

Cats are not always given this sorry role, however; in fact they are given a lot of affection as household pets, and they are considered to be attuned to subtle energies, so that their favourite places in the home are thought to be special spots for generating human wellbeing too. Owners note where their cats choose to sit or sleep, and follow suit. Other kinds of animals are also thought to have this gift, and a tradition practised in Siberia, decrees that the family should send their cow into a new home first, and note the place that it chooses to settle down in. This is then considered the most propitious for family members too. From Siberia as well comes another divination practice for a new house, whereby the householder throws four loaves of bread inside, one after the other. The way they fall signifies what kind of luck the family will have there; a loaf landing the right way up means good fortune. Perhaps this is linked to the Siberian shamanistic tradition, in which the four quarters of a ritual space are marked with small balls of baked dough.[1]

The human world of the izba

The traditional Russian house is known as an *izba,* which strictly speaking means the heated part of the home, the main dwelling rooms which can be inhabited all year round. (Any unheated rooms and adjacent storage areas are called the *seni.)* The word *izba* is an ancient one, possibly from pre-historic Germanic roots, and may therefore indicate that this type of house originates far back in time. The pattern of building and laying out the home has kept its essential features over the years. Even though today's village house is sure to have electricity and a television, and probably a fridge and a comfortable three-piece suite as well, it will almost certainly retain its traditional layout, a template which is rich in significance and custom (see Fig. 2).[2]

I will return to the overall construction of the house and how it is built later in the chapter, but for now will explore its interior, and the meaning of these three storeys of the home. The main living area of the home, where most of the sleeping, living and eating is conducted, is the easiest place to start. This is the ground floor, and corresponds to the middle level of the three storeys, representing the human world, which is neither down in the underworld nor up in the heavens.

As you enter the Russian home, you may have to stoop low as you pass through the doorway. This is deliberately done, so that anyone entering must show respect for the house, and in particular for the Red Corner, the sacred area of the home where the family icon is kept. Traditionally, the icon stands here on a high wooden corner shelf, draped with an embroidered linen towel, and often lit by a small votive lamp (see Fig. 20). To understand the place of icons in Orthodox culture, we need to know that they are not just religious images, but are considered to be holy objects, empowered in their own right as a gateway to the divine. They are painted according to specific rules, in ways that are believed to capture the essential lineaments of the divine spirit. Icons can represent saints and apostles, but in a domestic setting are likely to depict Christ, or Mary, Mother of God. The household icon is the main focus of family prayers. It can also be used in religious ceremonies, so that at a family wedding, for instance, it may be held over the young couple by the priest as they receive his blessing. But the icon is also a charged symbol that represents the welfare of the family itself. At the time of the Kursk submarine disaster in the year 2000, an old woman interviewed on television sobbed bitterly as she talked about her grandson, who was trapped at the bottom of the ocean: 'The icon fell off the wall a few days ago,' she sobbed. 'That is a bad, bad sign.'

The Red Corner, *krasni ugol,* is thus called because the colour red means 'beautiful' in Russian culture. The word *krasni* for red comes from the same root as the word for beautiful, *krassivi.* (It usually comes as a shock to realize that Red Square in Moscow has the same meaning — although it is, in fact, a very attractive square. And as for the Red Army ...) This is a pre-Christian Slavic tradition, and the ceremonial linen towels are embroidered in red also for this reason, that the colour is considered sacred, and represents not only beauty, but the force of life itself. The same towel that may be embroidered with figures of the Mother Goddess, the tree of life, and sky spirits in the form of horses, is used to drape the family icon in the mark of deepest respect. Once again, it is plain that there are few boundaries between the Christian and the indigenous Slavic symbolism in Russia.

The polarity of Christian and native religion also reveals itself in the layout of the room. Diagonally across from the Red Corner, and in opposition to it, is the place where the stove often stands, the *pechka* that is also known as 'the Little Mother'. The Orthodox icon guarantees a link with the heavenly rites of Byzantium, the stove with the elemental crucible of life itself. Without *pechka,* there is no life in the home; she is the source of warmth and comfort that may actually keep the family alive during the long Russian winters. A Russian proverb, which literally translates as, 'To dance from the stove', means 'To begin at the beginning': the stove is the origin and the perpetuator of life, and has associations too with the womb and gestation. Sometimes, in days gone by, a sickly or weak newborn child was put in the warming oven of the stove to 'bake', (at a suitable temperature, of course), in the belief that the stove would 'finish' the child's gestation and help it to become strong.

The *pechka* is multi-purpose, nurturing the family in various ways as a good mother does. Not only is it used for heating the home and for cooking, but traditionally it was also the place for sleeping. The classic construction of the stove is as a large box shape, constructed out of brick with a plaster finish; its flat top, six feet or so below the ceiling, provides an excellent sleeping platform. An artist in the lacquer miniature village of Kholui told me how he came to study there as a young man, taking lodgings with an old lady who gave him a space to sleep on top of the stove, along with a couple of other students as well! In old-fashioned homes, cloths would be hung around the sleepers on the stove, protecting them from the gaze of evil demons.

The stove requires skill and patience to manage. In the village house that I owned in the same village of Kholui, I knew that I had to listen and learn carefully when I was given instructions on how to light it, or my stays there in winter would be icy. I learnt how to leap out of bed on a frosty morning, and place pieces of kindling wood in the small metal firebox, igniting them with strips of dry birch bark that I had carefully peeled off the logs. When a blaze was going, I could open the dampers, add two or three split logs, and close the door of the fire box. Once that was alight, I would stoke the fire with a few more logs, then retreat back to bed with a cup of tea. But the critical stage of the operation was to wait observantly for the time when the logs had burnt down, and the tiny, residual blue flames had been replaced by an orange glow. Only then was it safe to close the dampers, and keep the heat in for another eight hours or so, the brick casing acting as a giant storage heater. Otherwise, deadly carbon monoxide can seep into the home, causing acute headaches or worse. I was saved from this once by a visitor to the house, who wrinkled his nose as he smelt the air, and promptly opened up the stove again and all the windows too. I never did master the skills of drying mushrooms or making porridge overnight in the cooler ovens of the stove, but I learnt to respect the life and death powers of the

'Little Mother', and to love her gentle, penetrating warmth.

The other key feature of the traditional living room is the dining table, and to sit there is to be 'in the palm of God', as the old saying expressively puts it. By tradition, it would be set under the Red Corner, and much of family life would be lived around this table. In older-style houses there was little extra furniture, and what there was, was plain and simple. More seating might be provided in the form of benches around the walls, which could also double up as guest beds or be used as workbenches for spinning, sewing, or craftwork.

The table was not only hallowed because of its proximity to the icon, but also because the very notion of hospitality in Russia is little short of sacred. If you are eating when a visitor knocks at the door, you must invite him or her to share your meal, insisting on it if necessary. Perhaps their arrival will be foretold; one of my guests dropped a knife on the floor as we were eating supper:

'Oh — a man is coming,' he told the assembled company.

'And what if it was a spoon?' I asked.

'Then it would be a woman.'

He was absolutely right; a male visitor knocked at the door before the meal was over. Although he had only come to deliver a message, we invited him to sit down with us, and coaxed him into accepting a small plateful of food and a glass of vodka, as custom demands.

In Russia, your relatives have *carte blanche* to turn up when they please, without prior notice, and to stay as long as they like. They may help with peeling potatoes and washing up, but they will also solemnly munch their way through three meals a day which the hosts have to provide at short notice. It is very rude to ask when they plan to leave. Traditionally, there was one way in which the hostess could tactfully indicate to her guests that it was time to go. She would bake small squares of gingerbread (known as *prianniki)* in a decorative mould, and distribute them when her food supplies were at an end. These were popularly known as 'get out' cakes, and if you were offered one of these, it was time to pick up your coat and bid farewell.

I made many mistakes of etiquette during my trips to Russia, and can only hope that people made allowances for my foreigner's ignorance. I was told sternly never to shake hands over a threshold, as I approached my host, hand eagerly outstretched, since this brings bad luck. I also discovered that an invitation to drink tea, or merely to call on someone, usually involves a large meal. Food must be served to guests on arrival, and plenty of it, so I was astonished several times over, before I learnt better, to enter a house and see the dining table laden with *zakuski* as *hors d'oeuvres,* bottles of vodka standing at the ready, and cutlery laid out implying soup and meat courses to come.

Meals are protracted, everyone keeping a little on their plates, and frequently helping themselves to just a spoonful or two more, so that the conversation will be prolonged and the glow of hospitality continue to warm the company. This is helped along by toasts, which are a part of every sociable meal. They are drunk to the hosts, to the guests, to *lubov',* or love, to friendship, and to whatever flights of fancy the proposer conjures up as the spirit of the occasion blooms. Glasses must be clinked, a process known as *chokanie.* Each glass must touch every other glass, and if you can't quite reach the glass of someone down the far end of the table, then it's a good idea to stand up and stretch over to *choknytsia* if you can. This friendly custom is said to have a more sinister origin; back in the days of warring knights, two rivals drinking together would clash their tankards so as to make a few drops from each vessel spill into the other. Thus the risk of being poisoned by the enemy was greatly reduced.

Everyone is encouraged to make a toast or two, and the Russian custom demands that a shot of vodka is downed in one to bring about the good fortune that is proposed. (They do not, however, smash their glasses as is popularly believed abroad.) Even a simple cup of tea, drunk in the family, involves everyone coming to the table, and sitting in convivial fashion. Nor must anything be drunk without eating, so while a glass of vodka includes a piece of bread and cucumber as an absolute minimum, a cup of tea always extends to confectionary, biscuits or a slice of cake. The custom of hospitality even extends to Russian television chat shows, where the host and his guest usually sit at a kind of contrived dining table, with a bowl of fruit or snacks between them, and a cup of tea or a soft drink at their elbow. In my viewing experience, they never touch the refreshments, but must have them there for show, since no conversation could be complete without them.

The *samovar,* or 'self boiler' as the word translates, is also a key part of Russian hospitality. It is sometimes seen as another symbol of the mother, along with the *pechka* and the Matrioshka doll. Its comforting curves, its decorative and gleaming brass, nickel or silver finish, and its near-boundless supply of hot water, make it a natural centrepiece for the tea table (see Fig. 5). Traditional samovars, as opposed to modern electrical ones, are heated by means of lighting a bundle of sticks or some charcoal in the central funnel, which then in turn heats up the water in the large outer chamber. The tea itself is made separately, in extra-strong quantities in a small teapot; a tiny amount of this brew is poured into each cup, which is then topped up with hot water from the samovar itself. Samovars are still popular, and large versions are often used in hotels and offices as well as at home. But, as a friend told me: 'The best kind of samovar is the kind that you light with charcoal and twigs, and add herbs to as well. You can sit outside in the garden, breathing in the fragrant steam and having a cup of tea every now and then; it is happiness that lasts for hours.'

So the Russian tradition is not made up simply of 'hard' folkloric evidence; it is the atmosphere created by following the customs handed down through families, the magic distilled within everyday living, such as taking tea from the samovar in the garden of the *dacha* (the Russian country or holiday home) on a warm summer's afternoon.

The best known ritual of hospitality in Russia is the welcoming ceremony known as 'Bread and Salt', *khlebsol.* A round loaf is used, in which a little hollow has been scooped out to hold a mound of salt; the loaf is placed on one of the long, embroidered linen towels, and offered to guests on arrival. Each person tears off a little of the bread, and dips it in the salt before consuming it (see Fig. 19). This is a symbol that the host and hostess are willing to share their food and their home with the newcomer. Although the custom of Bread and Salt doesn't take place on a regular basis these days, it is still often carried out at weddings, when the new bride enters the home of her mother-in-law. It may also be staged to welcome foreigners, for instance when a visiting dignitary arrives on Russian soil, or when tourists call at a country town on a river cruise.

Journeys themselves require hospitality and ritual. Russians are a people who are often on the move, whether visiting their country *dacha* at the weekend, or embarking on a long trek to see distant relatives.[3] In times gone by, this would have been an awesome undertaking, travelling through forests, across lakes, and along lonely tracks. Bears and wolves could pose a threat, and in winter there was the hazard of blizzards and the challenge of travelling along frozen rivers by horse-drawn sleigh. In modern times, there are different challenges, such as trying to sleep on creaking, smelly long distance buses, or dealing with a car breakdown in a remote area. There are modern dangers too, such as the seriously risky main roads where accidents frequently happen, and bandits rob passing cars and lorries. It is not surprising then, that travellers are welcomed now as in days of old, with a hearty meal and a warm berth for the night. And when visitors or family members set out on a journey, a solemn moment is required to bless their travels with good fortune.

'We'll all sit down together now,' said Ala, my hostess in St Petersburg, as I brought my suitcase into the hall, and prepared to leave for England. I was puzzled, but followed her into the living room, and took my place with the family there on one of the upright dining chairs. 'Now lift your feet off the floor,' she commanded us, 'and we'll sit in silence.' We sat quietly for a minute or two until she smiled, and declared the ritual complete. It would protect me on my journey, she said.

The underworld

After the bustling life on the ground floor of the house, the middle world, the descent into the cellar may seem dark and eerie. The cellar, or *podpol,* is a small room under the floor of the home, generally used as a place of storage, where root vegetables can be kept in a cool but even temperature through the winter, or big jars of marinated salad and home-made apple juice left until they are needed.[4] But in terms of traditional belief, it is much more than that. It is known as the place of the ancestors, and is often considered also to be the residence of the *domavoi,* or house spirit, a character who will shortly take centre stage.

In the Siberian shamanic culture, which almost certainly underlies the Russian magical worldview, the underworld is also the domain of the ancestors, and of other spirits besides. It is governed by an overlord, sometimes known as Erlik Khan. If a shaman endeavours to enter this lower realm as part of his trance journey, it is usually with an intention to bring back news from the ancestors, to predict the fortunes of the villagers for the year ahead, or even to find out which of their number might soon be departing into that lower world. Sometimes, too, the shaman-hero has to enter the underworld first in order to ascend to the higher worlds, touching the depths of the universe so as to rise to its heights. And just as the Russian house is a layered, physical representation of the spiritual universe, so Siberian shamans also have markers for these planes; they identify specific places in their local landscape which they believe have connections with each of the worlds. These places that represent the lower, middle or upper levels of the world are named by anthropologists as Cemetery, Settlement and Sanctuary respectively. Such a geographical feature could be a rock or cave at the base of a mountain signifying the entrance to the underworld, for instance, or a river heading towards the horizon seen as the gateway to the upper sky world. These landmarks are thought to have a material connection with the worlds of spirit, but in shamanic rituals they may be 'visited' in a state of trance or vision rather than in physical reality.

Traces of this sacred geography remain in Russian culture, for example in the fairy tale known as *The Three Kingdoms,* in which the young prince sets out to find his mother, who has been abducted by a whirlwind. His uncle gives him an iron ball, a magic device which rolls on ahead along the ground, leading the prince to a steep mountain range. Here he finds a cave guarded by a heavy metal door that he must use all his strength to open. Once inside, he discovers a pair of iron claws which allow him to climb the mountain and reach the kingdoms of Copper, Silver and Gold at its summit.[5] The cave at the base of the mountain is clearly a parallel with the entrance to the underworld in shamanic terms, and the three kingdoms above may well represent three different levels of the upper world to which the shaman climbs in order to wrestle with the spirits or gain precious knowledge from them. Shamanic cosmology is complex, and the three main levels or 'storeys' of the world are often further subdivided, so that it is quite normal, for instance, to have 'three kingdoms' contained within the sky world itself.

The underworld, both in shamanism and in Russian folk tradition, is often a realm of reversals, so that what is broken here in the human world becomes complete in the world below, for instance. If you break a glass, then your ancestors will be delighted to have one more glass to drink from down under. It is also sometimes known as a place of change or 'ripening', a 'posthumous refuge' for the departed as they await some form of new life.[6] The reversal can also be a spatial one, so that the bottom sphere of life may switch over to become the top one, and vice versa. Horizontal can suddenly become vertical, and vertical horizontal. This is a fascinating, if dizzying, topic in its own right, that need not concern us too much here, but something of this idea of abrupt change and reversal is retained in the tradition of the Russian homestead. A type of Russian wizard, a shape-shifter known as *oboroten* (*oborot* literally means the opposite, or reverse), is said to effect his transformation into another shape or creature by going into a cellar, where he turns a somersault to invoke the magical change (Kosarev 1999, p.5). And the Russian house spirit, *domavoi,* sometimes transfers himself instantaneously from cellar to attic, a place where he is not welcomed by humans, and from whence he has to be banished back to the lower regions again.

Domavoi's name comes from *dom,* the Russian word for house, and he is one of the tribe of Russian spirits known as 'nature spirits'. These nature spirits are often considered to be descended from former Slavic gods, but in my view they may be spirits of the elements, home and landscape that have long existed in their own right. They are temperamental, elusive, and tricky to deal with. They are akin in many ways to the mischievous 'elementals' of the Western magical tradition, or to the pixies and sprites of Western folklore. Russian nature spirits are not usually individually named, but they are specific to one location, so that each forest will have its own *leshi,* or forest spirit, and sometimes a Mrs *Leshi* and her children too. A *domavoi* is actually associated with a family rather than a house, and any family that moves house may have a difficult time ahead if they do not persuade their *domavoi* to come with them. One tried and tested method is to coax him into a sack, carry the sack to the new abode and then quickly offer *domavoi* a plate of porridge to help him settle down.[7] Another is to cut a thick slice of bread and place it under the stove in the new dwelling.

It is important to invite *domavoi* to come with you; even if he is capricious, the family needs him to be there. One folk narrative relates what happened to a peasant who did not do this; he forgot to issue the crucial invitation, and lived to regret it. He built a splendid new house for himself and his family, but they got ill, and their livestock did not prosper there. Then the peasant discovered that their *domavoi* was still living in the ash heap at the old house, and neighbours told him that a strange whining sound was heard coming from the pile of ashes every night. The peasant sought advice from a local wizard experienced in these matters, who told him that *domavoi* was lamenting the way he had been abandoned. Following his instructions, the peasant went to the ash heap and offered *domavoi* some bread and salt as the ultimate symbol of hospitality, and begged him in the most heartfelt terms to accompany him to the new home. After this gracious entreaty, *domavoi* consented to change his residence, and from then on the peasant and his family regained their health and good fortune (Ivanits 1992, pp.172–3). *Domavois* can also get mixed up, and end up in each other's houses by accident, which always brings chaos, so in this case cunning means have to be employed to get them back in their rightful places.

Although *domavoi* is commonly associated with the ancestors, and with the cellar of the home, he also likes to sit in the stove, and sometimes in the attic, and can in fact appear anywhere that he chooses. In general, it is considered unlucky to see *domavoi,* for this can presage a death in the household. If you do see him, he should not be addressed as *domavoi,* but more often as 'master' or 'grandfather'. In various traditions it is common to avoid calling a magical creature by its real name; in Russia the bear is often referred to as *Mishka,* an affectionate nickname, rather than by its proper name of *Medved,* or 'honey knower'. (This is paralleled in English, where even today in equestrian terminology, the correct term for a white horse is 'grey', once the way of showing respect to the sacred white horse.) You need to know how to recognize *domavoi* too, as like most nature spirits, he can appear in various forms. He might appear in the shape of a tiny, wizened old man, covered in downy hair, or as a tall figure 'black as coal', or even as an animal or a bundle of hay.

There is a tradition that *domavoi* will appear to the family on their first night in their new home, and that they may judge the their coming fortunes by this encounter. According to one narrative, an elderly couple spent the first night in their new home lying awake in terror, as they waited for the approach of *domavoi.* Not only might he have bad news for them, but it was well-known that he had a nasty habit of trying to strangle the people that he visited. The old woman screamed in terror as she felt something heavy and furry land on her chest, only to discover that it was the family cat! But on further reflection, the couple decided that the cat *was* the *domavoi* on this occasion, and that as its fur was soft and warm, good fortune would follow.

Is the belief in *domavoi* obsolete? Some Russians may well regard it as a quaint old folk belief, but to others the presence of spirits in the home and landscape is very real. On the island of Kiji, in the far north of Russia, I asked a woman from the regional city of Petrozavodsk what she thought about the *domavoi.*

'Every summer I come to work with tourists here, and I live alone in one of the old wooden houses. Oh yes, *domavoi* certainly exists. When I sit in this dark house at night, I sometimes hear a knocking, or I hear someone singing a melody. And even when I know the house is empty, I sense that there is someone upstairs. This is undoubtedly the *domavoi.'*

And I find it curious that while I was delving into accounts of *domavoi* and his appearances the other day in order to write this chapter, suddenly things started to go wrong in the kitchen. I finished my work and came down to prepare the evening meal. A bowl of cooked rice slipped out of my hands, making a terrible mess as it scattered everywhere. Knives fell off the rack with a loud clatter, apparently of their own volition, and the remote control that my partner was using positively leapt from his grasp and crashed onto the floor! I could not help being reminded of an account of how *domavoi* appeared to one family following their Christmas Eve celebrations:

'About midnight a noise resounded in the room ... the whole family woke up, but didn't even dare to budge from fear. They saw that the *domavoi* was sitting on the table breaking spoons and smashing plates, and on the floor were scattered overturned chairs and broken bottles and goblets …' (Ivanits 1992, p.170.)

And here is a small postscript: I had just sat down to breakfast with my partner after correcting this section, when we were both startled to hear a loud knock come from the cupboard under the stairs. Thinking that one of the cats had got trapped in there, I opened the door to investigate. There was nothing to be seen. Except, perhaps, *domavoi?*

The attic and the upper world

Many Russian houses have an unheated attic room, used mostly in summer, and known as *svetelka* (a word that comes from 'light', as in sunlight) or *cherdak.* This is the closest room in the house to the sun, which is considered to be the overall protector of the home. Such an elevated environment was traditionally thought to be beneficial for young girls, and to guard their innocence. Unmarried sisters and their girlfriends might officially sit up here together to sew or spin, but it was also the place for divination, especially in matters of love. Here they might unbraid their hair, an action which would loosen the bonds of the everyday world, and invite the powers of magic in. While their mothers believed them to be safely occupied with spinning and needlework, they would try to see the faces of their future husbands by gazing into a mirror, or tell fortunes by dropping some melted wax into a bowl, and interpreting the shapes that it formed (see Fig. 22).

Within living memory, the women's tasks of spinning and weaving were key activities in country life, and discarded spin-

Fig. 1 — Seizing the Firebird, the magical bird of light. *(Lacquer miniature from Kholui.)* See p. 87.

Fig. 2 — A traditional wooden house, or *izba*, in the village of Kholui. See p. 45.

Fig. 3 — The fretwork windows are designed to keep evil spirits away from the home. See p. 64.

Fig. 4 — Journey to Siberia: holding the White Stone to receive its energy charge. See p. 7.

Fig. 5 — Old-style tea-drinking. *(Lacquer miniature from Fedoskino.)* See p. 50.

Fig. 6 — Fortune telling by cards. *(Lacquer miniature from Fedoskino.)* See p. 113.

Fig. 7 — Snowmaiden, delicate daughter of Father Frost and Mother Spring. *(Lacquer miniature from Kholui.)* See p. 158.

Fig. 8 — Herel, the Siberian shaman. See p. 93.

Fig. 9 — The doll effigy at the festival of Maslnitsa is paraded, and will finally be destroyed: Moscow, 2002. See p. 153.

Fig. 10 — A traditional country wedding; the celebrations often go on for three days. *(Lacquer miniature from Fedoskino.)* See p. 21.

Fig. 11 — Spinning from a distaff. See p. 57.

ЯГА БАБА ЕДЕТЪ СКОРКОДИЛОМЪ ДРАТИСЯ
НАСВИНЬЕСПЕСТОМЪ ДАУНИХ ЖЕПОКУСТОМЪСК
ЛАНИЦАСВИНОМЪ

Fig. 12 — The witch Baba Yaga does battle with a sorcerer-wolf. *(Traditional woodcut.)* See p. 103.

Fig. 13 — Birch bark, one of the most useful and ancient materials in Russia. See p. 131.

dles, distaffs and spinning wheels can still readily be bought at flea markets. It was not only a practical occupation, spinning flax or wool and weaving it into cloth for costumes, towels, hangings and bed linen, but also an activity that symbolized the bringing of order and civilization to the community (see Fig. 11). As we have already seen, Mokosh the mother goddess played a particular role in relation to spinning, and there was another female household spirit called Kikimora who also presided over distaff and loom. Kikimora was quick to punish any women who did not put their spinning and needlework away tidily at night, and it was a bad omen to come across Kikimora at her own spinning, a possible sign of one's impending death. She might, however, help out the diligent housewife by taking on some of her work at night (see Ivanits 1992, p.57 or *New Larousse*, p.290).

Distaffs were often highly decorated, painted in lively colours with human figures, animals, and geometric motifs, according to the style of the region (An example of decoding such motifs on a distaff is given on p.26.) Spinning was a symbol of safe, industrious activity for the unmarried girls of the household, and it was fondly believed by their parents that when their fingers were thus engaged, they could come to no harm. In summer they were sometimes allowed to go to parties, held perhaps in a house belonging to somebody's grandmother, who would tactfully withdraw while the young lads and girls of neighbouring villages had a chance to get to know each other. This was a social custom followed especially in the north of Russia, where villages might be too far apart and the climate too harsh for boys and girls to meet in the normal course of life. The northern houses were larger than average too, since extended families and their animals would all live under the same roof, and the houses would thus make excellent party venues. The girls were under strict instructions to work away with their distaffs and spindles while they conversed, which, in theory at least, performed the double function of keeping them out of mischief while at the same time showing the boys what good housewives they would make!

Just as the act of weaving and ordering the threads denotes the influence of human civilization, so the act of unbinding signifies the opposite, the opening of the gateway to magical forces. The attic has traditionally been a suitable place to do this, though not the only one, since the bath house too has its potent magic, as will shortly be revealed. The woven belt once worn around the waist by both men and women symbolized the participation of individuals in society, their place in the community, and the agreement to be, quite literally, bound by its rules. When the reverse was practised, taking off one's belt signified a readiness to enter the realm of the spirits. For women, the power could be amplified by unbraiding their hair, as mentioned above. Any kind of knot or binding was considered to have magical significance, and the Christian sect of the Old Believers still tie their scarves without knots, to show that they have no truck with magical practices of any kind.

The attic, therefore, could be a place both of light and innocence, and of magic, though it seems a lighter-hearted kind of magic than the deeper, more ominous, magic of cellar and bathhouse. The sky world is, after all, that of the heavens, and the top part of the house is often decorated externally to reflect this. In the Volga region especially, the protruding end of the ridgepole is frequently fashioned into a form of a horse, known in Russian mythology as a sky creature. Symbols of the sun, such as cockerels or circles with rays around them, and those which signify heaven, like peacocks and bunches of grapes, are commonly found carved into the upper part of the house façade, and boards covering the ends of the roof beams are commonly known as 'wings'.

The bathhouse

Of sky beliefs and celestial forces in the Russian tradition, there will be plenty to say in the next chapter. In the meantime, we shall visit the bathhouse. This has been an important part of Russian life since time immemorial, and the custom of weekly steam bathing in an extreme temperature was noted with surprise by early travellers to Russia, one of whom described it as 'a veritable torment'.[8] The bathhouse is more than a place to get clean on Saturday night, the traditional Russian day for bathing, and a choice of day apparently shared by the Vikings. It has been for centuries a place of ritual and magic, used for ceremonies on a wedding eve, and for childbirth; it is one of the most potent places for divination, and it is also the home of the *bannik,* a spirit even more mischievous than the *domavoi.* Although the type of bathhouse I am about to describe is from a domestic or village setting, the cult of the bathhouse has always been widespread, embraced by nobility and peasants alike; the *tsaritsa* gave birth in a bathhouse just like her serfs, and in modern Russian society today there are urban bathhouses which are used by sophisticated city dwellers.

The bathhouse is a house in miniature, built out of wood with a pitched roof and its own small chimney. It usually stands apart from the *izba* and is often found at the bottom of the vegetable garden, where there is least risk of fire. The fire that is lit in the iron stove of the bathhouse heats a cauldron or copper of water set within the stove, and also heats a quantity of large stones or bricks contained in a small inner chamber. The essential nature of the bathhouse is thus fire and water, the two elements that are considered to be natural enemies in magical practices.[9] The art of bathing there involves the skilful creation of steam to the required degree, by opening the chamber containing the hot stones and splashing boiling water onto them. There are various stages in the ritual, such as rinsing oneself with warm water (a tub of cold water also stands in the bathhouse, making provision for mixing hot and cold to any temperature required) and then lying for a while on one of the wooden benches or platforms before engaging in the more intense process of steaming. Switches of birch twigs (*venniki*) are used for one person to flick or whip another with; the sensation is light and stimulating, and far from painful! There is a traditional form of body massage using these *venniki,* and there is also a tradition that the birch should be cut in early summer, when at its most potent. The family whose bathhouse I used told me that they try to gather them around June 24, the old Russian midsummer festival. They showed me how they hang the bunches of twigs up to dry, complete with their leaves, which then can be used all year round. I was also taught how to steep a bunch of dried birch twigs in a bowl of tepid water, which gives an infusion whose delicate aroma perfumes the bathhouse, and which makes an excellent final rinse for a hair wash.

Sometimes special natural ingredients are added to the steam, such as herbs or essential oils, and these create fragrances that can be beneficial to health as well as intoxicatingly delicious to the senses. In a mountain forest camp and health clinic in Siberia, I also encountered the delights of the *fitobochka,* a kind of barrel bath. My companion and I took it in turn to sit in a large, upright barrel, perched on a little shelf about half way down, and covered over at the top so that only one's head and neck stick out. The feet rest on a wooden inner partition, separating the bather (thankfully) from the boiling steam in the lower chamber, piped in from another water boiler on the other side of the room. In this somewhat unnerving and undignified position one must sit for a long fifteen minutes, while the doctor sternly consults her pocket watch every couple of minutes to make sure that there is no cheating. The steam in the *fitobochka* is fed with selected herbs, plants and leaves, so that one is immersed in an intense herbal steam that gradually penetrates into the body, as well as encouraging the sweating and cleansing process that is the key feature of the Russian *banya* as well as the Siberian *fitobochka.*

In this case, the doctor was a middle-aged lady called Valentina. After our *fitobochka,* she told me how she had come to be a herbalist as well as a doctor. Under the Communist regime, it was common to send out students and young professionals each year for a spell on the land, and, each year, Valentina and her husband were sent out to help with the haymaking in a remote Siberian village. She became interested in the plants that she found, and discovered that the old ladies of the village still held a treasury of knowledge about herbal lore. Over the years, with their help, she developed expertise in the medicinal use of herbs, and she and other like-minded practitioners still glean knowledge from older inhabitants today, and share their findings in journals which are held by archivists in the local towns (see Fig. 25). As each herbalist discovers some fresh piece of information, he or she inscribes it into the journal, and the next colleague to visit the archive can consult the journal to see what new discoveries have been made; it is a remarkably effective and practical way of passing the word round in this wild terrain. Valentina claims proudly to have revived the ancient art of the *fitobochka,* and added some 'modern' refinements, perhaps mainly in the form of the red rubber sheets we were draped in, and the dodgy looking pipes from the boiler tank to the barrel.

The effects were wonderful, however. After the *fitobochka,* as after steaming in the *banya,* relaxation and replenishment of liquids is the order of the day. A thorough steam bath can leave one feeling light-headed, cleansed and refreshed, but also in a somewhat delicate condition; beer, soft drinks, tea or water are recommended, and the usual favourite tipple of vodka is strictly off limits till the effects of the bath have worn off. Two close English acquaintances of mine, who shall be nameless, decided that the rules were not for them, and downed a large quantity of vodka after a Russian Saturday night bath. Unused to the powerful effects of both bath and vodka, they became wildly inebriated, embarrassing their companions and surprising even their broad-minded Russian hosts with their unruly behaviour.

The bathhouse is inextricably bound up with magic and divination.[10] Any spell or charm is most potent when cast at midnight in the bathhouse. Anyone wishing to become a sorcerer is advised to seek initiation in the bathhouse, also best carried out at the witching hour of midnight (Ryan 1999, pp.50, 99). The role of the bathhouse is considered by some authorities to be that of a temple, a 'pagan' temple relegated to this warm and steamy place after the old religion was displaced from the heart of society by the coming of Christianity. The bathhouse is thus the place where some of the last vestiges of pre-Christian magic are preserved, and, in accordance with the practice of *dvoeverie,* or two faiths, it may form a polarity with the Red Corner of the home: 'In the little cosmos of each village household, then, the bathhouse stands at one, "pagan" spiritual pole; at the other is "the fine corner" ... of the main room of the house ... where the household icons would stand ...'[11]

The rituals carried out on the bride's wedding eve were always conducted in the bathhouse. This was an occasion for women only, usually with just the bride's girlfriends present, unless the sorcerer himself came to preside over the ceremony. The village sorcerer or wizard (*koldun*) was a genuine source of magical knowledge, and could act as diviner as well as conducting rituals, but he was also feared for his powers; this meant that he was often invited to the wedding as an insurance policy, so as to avoid any possibility that he might cast the Evil Eye on the nuptials, and spoil the luck of the young couple (Ryan 1999, p.75). When the wedding eve ceremony was ready to begin, the girls would remove the bride's belt and unbraid her hair—magical acts, as we have already seen but in this case also a ritual violation of the young woman's innocence and chastity, which she would then lament loudly in (ritual) protest. Once inside the bathhouse, she was carefully washed by her female friends. Everything was charged with meaning: the bathhouse fire was checked to see how it was burning, and the couple's future divined from this; a peaceful fire was a portent of married contentment. The water used to wash the bride was kept, to be used later for cooking of special dumplings or pies that would then be fed to the bridegroom, an extraordinarily sensual rite of passage to bind the couple together body and soul.[12] Girls hoping to marry would themselves take away some of the bathing water to ensure their luck in the future.

More playful versions of divination in the bathhouse for love still take place today. Girls set up a deliciously scary ritual, in which they go into the bathhouse one by one, into an atmosphere thick with steam, and feel around until they touch someone's hand. The type of touch they encounter tells them what kind of husband they will marry — if it's a hairy hand, he will be rich, if smooth then he will be poor, and if wet, he will certainly be a drunkard![13] This touch is meant to be that of the spirit of their future husband, but in practice the game is often aided and abetted by the local boys, who enjoy taking a turn to hide in the bathhouse and frightening each of the girls in turn.

The bannik

The spirit of the bathhouse is known as the *bannik*. Like most Russian domestic spirits and nature spirits, he is a shape-shifter, who can change his appearance at will. For much of the time, he is not seen at all, since he owns a cap of invisibility, but when he does choose to show himself, he might appear in the form of a large black cat, or perhaps as an old man with a green beard. *Bannik* can also manifest as a heavy stone or a burning coal, so potentially he could be around in the bathhouse at any time, making it a place of menace as he is bad-tempered, and brooks no breach of etiquette. Students working on Kiji Island during their summer break told me that they always treated *bannik* with great respect. One of their number, an intellectual young man who thought he knew better, refused to ask *bannik's* permission to enter the bathhouse as required, and neglected to leave a little offering of soap or a fir twig for the bath spirit as is the accepted custom. The next time he entered the bathhouse, he tripped over, dropped his glasses, and trod on them by mistake. Stooping down to retrieve the now broken glasses, he stood up too abruptly and cracked his head on a low beam. Since then, his friends reported, he has always shown the proper respect to the spirit of the bathhouse.

The bathhouse has always been considered a dangerous place, where malevolent spirits may lurk. It is, or was, the place to give birth, but a new mother must not be left alone there in case unclean spirits might be drawn to her, or try to steal the baby. If a bathhouse burnt down, then a black hen would be buried on the threshold to placate *bannik* and ameliorate the misfortune. It was a place too where a person could be confronted with his or her approaching death, through a vision or some form of divination. Potent, risky, pagan, but also a great source of pleasure to almost every Russian today, the bathhouse retains its position in the heritage of Russian traditional culture and magic.

The house and its decoration

Now that all the essential components of the Russian house have been described, I would like to take a final look at its construction, and also at how it is decorated, inside and out. The *izba* is usually built of logs, and the image of the axe and the house go together. The phrase 'to build a house' in Russian actually means 'to hew a house'. Building an *izba* is usually a family affair, a time when neighbours and relatives in the village are roped in to help measure, cut and erect the logs into the form of a square or rectangle, forming the outer shell of the house. When I owned an *izba* in the artists' village of Kholui, one of the old masters of the lacquer miniature painting school there used to drop in every now and then, looking the place over once again and nodding his head with gentle satisfaction. 'I remember when I helped to build this,' he would say, as the previous owners had been friends of his and they had all worked together on the house. The logs are carefully numbered and recorded as they are moved into position, so that if the house starts to sink into the boggy ground (a common occurrence) it can be dismantled and propped up again. It has even been known for people to take their houses with them when they move. There is an intimate bond between the owner and the self-built house, which links the Russian country-dweller not only to the creation of his or her home, but also to the forest itself, which is the source of so much in Russian life and culture (see Chapter 6).

There is an intense love of colour and decoration in Russia, and the country is rich in arts and crafts, some of which are widespread, and some which are regional in origin. Houses are often decorated on the outside with wooden carvings, as already mentioned, and home owners compete with each other to create the finest of these. As well as those representing the sun or sky symbols in the upper parts, there may be carvings of lions or mermaids to protect the home, birds to symbolize happiness, and beautiful descending panels of fretwork on the front wall, imitating the embroideries on the ceremonial linen towels. The exotic creatures, like the lions and mermaids, may once have started out as figureheads on ships; the town of Gorodets, for instance, has a long history of producing ships' carvings of this type. The most prominent and typical decorative feature of the *izba* is the carving around the windows, lacy window frames known as *nalichniki,* which incorporate a variety of motifs, often rosettes or floral designs, and sometimes even the Communist five-pointed star. There are two schools of thought about the origin of this custom. One is that this fretwork carving has always been a way of protecting the home, by guarding the windows against the entry of evil spirits. The other view is that the unmarried daughters of the house look exceptionally pretty as they sit sewing at the window, framed by such delicate and decorative carving, and would thus readily catch the eye of any eligible young man strolling by! (see Fig. 3)

In some regions, houses are painted internally with bright motifs. The artist Kandinsky became very interested in these, as he did in other traditional forms of Russian and shamanic belief, and they all had a profound influence on his own paintings. Although the designs of these decorations may appear to be quite simple, they can actually be full of meaning, reflecting the cosmological pattern that governs the building of the house as a whole. One example of such a home, from the Urals region, has a living room that is painted in three tiers or levels, echoing the three worlds of sky, earth and underworld, according to those who have studied it. On the ceiling, which represents the sky, a circular solar motif is painted; the middle of the walls depict nature in full bloom, representing the world around us, and the lower level is painted as an imitation of marble, signifying the underground kingdom (Krasunov 1996, p.25).

Craft forms are an intrinsic part of traditional life. In the home, crafts would be taken up during the long winter evenings, and the whole family might get to work on painting, carving or embroidery. Certain crafts often began in specific localities; it was common, for instance, for families living near a place of pilgrimage to carve wooden figures or spoons to sell to the visitors. Often the children made the blank wooden spoon, the father carved and refined it, and the mother gave it a painted finish, sometimes decorating it with a proverb or initials. Spoons were not merely humble household objects, but played a part in traditional rituals, such as the custom of using two spoons knotted together by a single thread to symbolize union in wedding celebrations. This tradition of local craftwork still continues in Sergev Posad, not far from Moscow, where Matrioshka dolls and dancing wooden bears are on sale to the thousands of pilgrims and tourists who visit the monastery there.

Other towns and villages developed their own regional craft specialities, which may have simply evolved from craftsmen and families sharing their skills. In the village of Zhostovo, also in the Moscow region, metal trays are skilfully painted in oils with richly coloured bouquets of flowers, and in the town of Gorodets, near Nizhni Novgorod, delightful naïve scenes are painted on wooden ware for the home. The mythic version of the birth of such crafts, however, is that as the magical Firebird flies over the land, every now and then she lets fall one of her feathers, each one of which is brilliant with light. Wherever it lands, a new artistic tradition will spring up. This tale is told about the origin of Khokhloma ware, which is described below; the Firebird herself is a creature of light and inspiration, as we shall see in the next chapter.

Whatever their history, some regional craft forms became highly sophisticated, and the most prominent were collectivized under Soviet rule. This had the virtue of keeping the arts and crafts going during an increasingly industrialized period. The craftsmen and women were paid a salary, and worked usually in a large, factory-like building, where, for instance, the making of the basic forms, such as papier-mâché for lacquer miniature boxes, or the turning of wood for nesting dolls, was done by artisans in the nether regions, while the artists occupied light and airy studios on the top floor, where they could concentrate on delicate decoration or the painting of fairy tale scenes. Very often, a teaching school was established in the village to train up a new generation, and a museum housed the best of the tradition, a place where students could study the work of past masters, and visitors could admire a showcase of their work. These institutions still exist in various craft centres, and in various stages of privatization, but their future is precarious in changing, post-Communist times.

There is a great range of Russian crafts; some are very simple, but others, like the lacquer miniatures, can be a complex art form in their own right. Working in tempera or oil paint, the artists create exquisite scenes of fairy tales, landscapes or village scenes on papier-mâché boxes, which are then lacquered to finish. One of the reasons for the great success of the lacquer miniatures is that they draw deeply on the resources of Russian fairy tale and legend, so that the work has a mythic quality that draws one into its heart. Their work is hailed as some of the best miniature painting in the world today, and is bought by collectors world-wide, as well as filling many show-cases in Russian museums, although the expertise and time needed to create a miniature has priced them out of the range of the average Russian family.[14]

It is typical, however, to find at least one or two craft items in almost every Russian home. Perhaps this is due to a deep-seated desire to keep the connection with the folk art tradition, or perhaps it is a way of introducing extra colour or artistic interest into the home. One of the most popular crafts in this respect is Khokhloma ware. Wooden bowls, spoons, boards, cups and vases, to mention but a few of the items, are turned from wood, then painted with decorative patterns, primarily in black, red and gold (see Fig. 21). The gold is actually made from a silvery powder (powdered tin, or silver chloride), which is brushed on to the surface as and where needed, and then heated gently in an oven, where it turns into a golden colour. This technique has long been admired, and is the subject of a few legends. One concerns an icon painter in days gone by, who understood this secret of 'making' gold. But rather than pass it on to anyone else, he set fire to himself and his home, planning to take the secret with him. After the fire had burnt itself out, however, people found that the house itself was now golden, as a result of firing the powder, and managed to work out the secret for themselves.

The colours of black, red and gold that predominate in Khokhloma ware have their own special significance.

'These three colours bring harmony to the human soul,' said the director of the studio as he showed us the gorgeous array of work in their museum. Each piece was painted with individually created designs of ferns, flowers and berries, all stylized into meandering, branching shapes, with graceful flourishes and swirling patterns. 'The psychologists have tested this combination of colours, and find that they are the only three colours which people can gaze at for a long time without feeling restless or disturbed.'

Furthermore, he told us, each of the colours has its own meaning. 'Red is for life, and energy,' he said. 'Black is for suffering. But it is also for compassion, for when people share their sorrows then they truly find that compassion for each other. And gold —gold is for hope, and for eternal life.'

Gold is the magic ingredient in Khokhloma ware, and it is also the symbol of eternity and the other world in fairy stories, both in Russia and in other traditions. So perhaps it is the chief colour in this trinity, even though it is the one used most sparingly.

The information that was given to us on this occasion shows that not only do colour and decoration have great meaning in traditional Russian culture, but also that in the modern era, Russians themselves have reflected on this meaning, and drawn it out consciously. This was not an isolated example, as I have seen, heard and read many times how attuned Russian people are to perceiving symbolic and spiritual meaning in their customs and in their art forms.

Colour, craft and decoration put the finishing touches to the Russian home, and it is in the detail of the home that we can discover much of the old Russian worldview, and also a sense of the Russian soul. Great literature and music are not the only places to discover Russian spirituality, and in fact they themselves are often founded on the mythology and traditional cosmology of the Russian people, as in the case of Pushkin's fairy tales, or Stravinsky's ballets.[15]

The Slavic contrast

So far, the house described has been small-scale, built around the needs of a family and their livestock, and capable of accommodating guests and relatives under its roof. But anyone who has been to Russia will know that there are many buildings created on a huge scale, and that the cities are full of high-rise blocks. The dictator Stalin left seven monumental, ziggurat style edifices scattered around the city of Moscow to make his mark, which still dominate the skyline today. Hotels are gigantic, more like small cities in themselves, with a bounden duty to provide everything from a doctor to a hairdresser, even if this is more honoured in theory than in practice. This defines another intrinsic polarity of Russian culture, the small and homely versus the huge and forbidding. I pondered over this question of size, wondering why Russians build so large until, one evening in Moscow, I came upon a scene that satisfied my curiosity, and gave me one possible answer to the puzzle. I wrote this in my diary at the time:

> Coming home at midnight to the hotel, I saw the new wooden towers of Izmailovo market silhouetted against the swirl of snow.[16] The sky was greyish and faintly lit by the lamps around. They've been building a kind of wooden village or fortress there, garnished with carved statues, Old Russian fantasy style. I'd seen it many times before, but with the towers looming out of the snowy

darkness it made me catch my breath. One of them suddenly looked in silhouette like one of Stalin's towers. Then, in my perception, it was quickly replaced by a likeness of the Kremlin towers around the walls, and I realized for the first time that they were similar in source, Stalin's buildings and the Moscow Kremlin. And then that in turn gave way to an image of the old wooden fortress towers of Russia from medieval times, and even earlier as pre-Christian Slavic stockades. Suddenly, I was aware of the line running through it all. It was, and still is, a way of making a mighty statement in a dark, cold, snowy land. I could imagine approaching those towers with awe, arriving from a long and desolate journey and seeing them loom up in front of me. The towers will keep the inhabitants in awe too, yet they'll think of it as their own, their people's achievement. It goes a long way to explaining the ongoing Russian urge to build huge.

4

Spirits of the Sky

O Sun, bright Sun
As you wander round the world,
And protect the earth from evil,
So protect our kind from evil and want.
Rise, Sun, over our yard, to our bread-and-salt!

The sky is a living world in the Russian tradition. Sun, Moon and stars are seen as animate, and even wind and weather are recognized as active spirits. The lords of the sky interact with the human world, sometimes benevolently, bestowing fruitfulness and good fortune, at other times fiercely, searing the land and blasting away hope. The sky is the uppermost of the three world levels in old Russian cosmology, and it is the place where ultimate judgment resides, but also where ultimate happiness may come from.

Russian lore and tales tell us that people can engage with these celestial spirits, and even use native wit to get the best of them, but they always make the point that the powers of the sky must always be respected, or bad luck will surely follow. They indicate that there is an active dialogue between the worlds; humans want to communicate with the upper realms, and even to visit them, but often they need help to do so. Traditionally, this assistance can come from certain creatures who are intermediaries between sky and earth. These include messenger birds, which fly to and fro between the worlds, and horses that can leap up from one world to another, magical beings who we will meet later on in this chapter.

Sun and Moon

Above all reigns the Sun; the Sun is the lord of the heavens, and just as it rules supreme in the sky, so this golden orb must be honoured first and foremost in the human world too. Many calendar customs were created in deference to the Sun, and in marking its journey through the year.

On the morning of January 2 each year, villagers would tread a path around their homes, chanting the rhyme above to welcome the return of the Sun. After the deep darkness of the winter solstice, the days were about to lengthen, and in due course, the Sun's rays would penetrate the harsh cold and the frozen land. All must be prepared, so that the year could move smoothly forward; snow would be shaken off the apple trees on this day too, to ensure a good harvest. This ritual was known as 'The Sun's Path', and the circle trodden around the home was a deliberate invocation of the circle of the Sun's path during the year. It was said of the old way of Russian life: 'They lived in the woods and worshipped the wheel', signifying how the basic resources for life were found in the forest, but how all was made possible by the cycle of the year, for which due reverence was paid to the Sun (Rozhnova, pp.15 & 35). The image of the Sun as a moving circle was depicted many times over in folk design, symbolized by wheels, rosettes, and swastikas.

In Russian belief, the Sun is all-seeing, and only the truth must be told under its rays. On January 7, according to folk custom, the Sun is expected to shine, and you may ask the person you care for: 'Do you love me?' But only do so if you are brave enough to learn whether your affections are returned, for on this day, as the Sun's power is waxing once more, only an honest answer must be given.

The Sun is also a protector of the house, so that a good array of Sun symbols created about the home would guard and guide the family. These too should be of the Sun in motion, such as a 'walking' Sun embroidered on a towel, or a 'rolling' Sun carved on a lintel. The images themselves would be considered to contain something of the Sun's power, so that the towel could bring healing when used to wipe the sick person's face, and the carved Sun on the house front would help to drive away severe weather.

The great Sun Festival is Maslnitsa, which is still popular today, and to which we shall return in the final chapter. It is the Russian equivalent of Shrovetide in the Christian calendar and thus marks the start of Lent, but most of its elements are drawn from the old spring festivals; round pancakes symbolizing the wheel of the Sun are eaten, and the image of Yarilo, the old Sun God, smiles from souvenir booths as a golden disc made out of straw, with orange flames emerging from his beaming countenance. Hang this reminder of the Sun God in your home, and perhaps the deity will bless you in the year to come.

As well as being cheerful and benevolent, Yarilo is in a position of authority too, and holds the power to command the change of seasons. On March 2, he inspects the farmers' ploughs to see if they are ready for work, while on March 3 he orders the yellow bunting to start singing, a solar bird itself with its golden plumage. Yarilo is also depicted as a being of white-hot passion, who is fierce in battle, warring against the darkness and cold of winter. Some authorities see him as a protagonist in the primal battle between darkness and light, and identify this struggle as another mythic binary opposition in Russian culture (see p.12). In oral tradition too, there are hints of another kind of duality, the notion of two Sun deities, comprising the risen and the set Sun, which each inhabit their own worlds. This is an ancient cosmology going back at least to the Bronze Age, according to drawings found on pottery of that period, which has survived into our own era (Warner 1985, p.51).

But this image of the Sun as a masculine warrior is only one of the traditional views; the Sun is in fact very often represented as feminine in Slavic mythology. As invoked in an old funeral lament, she may be known as 'the fair maiden Bright Sun', who in this case will assist the soul as it flies upwards in the form of a white swan, to find its final rest in her arbour. There are many beautiful and imaginative tales told about the Sun, such as that of a solitary traveller who travels far away to the place where sky and earth meet. Here he knocks on the door of a cottage to ask for shelter, only to discover that it is the home of Bright Sun, a beautiful girl wearing a radiant, shimmering robe, with wings like those of an angel. Each evening, when she returns from her journey through the sky, her old mother gives her food, and then helps her to take off her robe and her glowing wings, thus causing darkness to fall. At dawn, she dresses her daughter again, and bids her goodbye as the maiden flies away once more to cast light from the skies.

Sometimes both sexes are present in solar myth, so that, for instance, the Sun himself may be masculine, but his daughters are the sunbeams that create the play of light and shadow on the earth. In one Siberian tale, for instance, Father Sun has three daughters, whose names are Golden Sunshine, Misty Shadow and Bright Sunbeam. Stories about Sun, Moon and stars seem to have been especially popular in Siberia, perhaps because of a nomadic way of life, which would give people greater exposure to the sight of the stars, Sun and Moon, and encourage them to perceive these as characters in the cosmic drama. Old stories would have been passed down, and new tales woven and embroidered like the starry canopy above, as people sat around the fire on dark evenings.

Where the Sun is seen as feminine, the Moon is usually considered to be masculine, and the pair may be identified as brother and sister, or as lovers. Tales are related of how they came to take their places in the sky, and why they have the appearance that they do. One story, *The Sun Maiden and the Crescent Moon,* again from Siberia, begins with the Sun as a lonely girl in the sky, who is longing for a handsome lover. An equally lonely man wanders the plain below, looking up every now and then and sighing as he admires the beauty of the Sun above. Sun Maiden has very long arms, and she just manages to take hold of the man and lift him up into the sky to be with her. They live happily together for a while as husband and wife, but it is too hot for the man, and he begs to return to earth for a short break. Sun Maiden provides him with a winged horse so that he can fly down again to his home, but on his return to the human world, a wicked sorceress plots against him. As the Sun Maiden attempts to rescue him by reaching down from heaven, the sorceress holds on grimly to her captive, and finally between them, they pull the poor man apart so that he is split into two pieces. The half remaining in Sun Maiden's grasp is cold, for his heart is left behind in the other part.

She sends him then to the far end of the sky, to its darkest corner, with the words: 'From this day forth we shall be parted and see each other only on the longest day of the year; even then it will be no more than the merest glimpse.' He remains there at the end of the sky as the Crescent Moon, his rays cold and lifeless, and from then until the present day, he and Sun Maiden can only see each other on the longest day of the year (Riordan 1989, p.55).

Dark nights and starry skies

In Russia, people seem to be in tune with twilight and the approach of nightfall in a way that is not common in the West. I have been gently chided on various occasions for turning on the electric light too quickly in the evening; my Russian friends prefer to move around in the half-light, or sit and enjoy the gentle dusk. As night comes on, it is the custom to take a stroll if the weather is fine and to admire the moon and stars. *Provodit'* is a verb that means to accompany someone on foot, and in a village setting, is often invoked after supper, when the hosts announce that they will see their guests home. Everyone ambles back along the path, linking arms, and singing too if the mood is mellow. If it is a warm summer's evening, sometimes the sound of other music and laughter may be heard floating across the fields or river, where an impromptu party is taking place, and the *garmon'*, an instrument like a small accordion, is accompanying an airing of favourite folk songs like 'Oh Frost, Frost!' or 'Katusha'. In the distance, a glow of light can be seen from the party-goers' bonfire, becoming ever more intense as the darkness deepens.

This is quintessential Russian life, and the respect for twilight, and the walking of guests home in the evening, occurs to some degree in the city just as it does in the country. Perhaps this evening activity indicates that there is still a lingering sense of the magic which is traditionally associated with darkness; in Russia, the dark has always been the proper time for telling stories and 'wonder tales', whose enchantment is heightened if they are related after sunset.

Clear winter nights have their own magic too. One New Year's Eve, while staying in my wooden *izba* in the artists' village of

Kholui, I left the snug warmth there to brave the cold evening air, invited to join friends for their annual family party. New Year's Eve is more of a family occasion than it is in the West, so it was an honour to be asked to join them. However, the temperature was something like twenty-nine degrees Celsius below, and the night was so cold that my breath froze in my nostrils as I stepped out. But I forgot the cold when I found that the moonlight was playing on the frozen snow, and, to my amazement, I saw that every snow crystal around me flashed like a diamond or precious jewel as the light caught it. I was at once transported to the fairy tale of *Silver Hoof,* a story from the Ural Mountains.[1] This is a fable of a little deer who lives deep in the forest, who lets loose a shower of crystals and gems whenever he stamps his foot. In the story, he visits an old man and his little granddaughter, and unleashes a cascade of jewels on the roof of their snowbound hut. As I watched the snow sparkle with red, green and white light, I could see it as a field of gemstones, each one a tiny exquisite miracle. Moon, frost and jewels were connected in a triad of beauty, and the legend now made perfect sense to me.

Stars, too, play their part in Russian magical lore. One night, after a cheerful and sociable supper gathering in the same village, *provodit'* was in progress, as we were all strolling back to my house in the time-honoured fashion. By the bridge over the river, we stopped to admire the sky, brilliant with stars.

'Look! A shooting star!' I said.

'*Zhelanye!*' Pyotr and Olga, the hosts, spoke as one. 'Wish! Make a wish!'

There was a moment's silence as we each searched our hearts for the wish that we wanted to make, and then we carried on our way, laughing and chatting. Thus I discovered that British and Russian people have at least one tradition in common where stars are concerned.

Other customs to do with stars are more specific to Russia, however, and some early star names from the pre-Christian era there have come down to us. The word *los,* meaning elk, was used for one star, and *kolo* (whose meaning is unknown) was the term given to the constellation Orion (see Ryan 1999, p.384). *Volosiny* was the name of the Pleiades, a constellation associated with the pre-historic cult of the bear, and which was probably named for the god Veles, a principal deity of the Slavic pantheon who ruled the annual bear hunt as well as being the lord of cattle. The position of the Pleiades in the sky may have been used as a celestial reminder of when to begin the hunt (see Haney 1999, p.68). The Pole Star was also identified in early Russian culture, and is described in one legend as a dog who is fettered to the sky. It struggles against its bonds, continually gnawing away at its leash, and when it finally breaks free, so the myth says, the world will end.

Stars are said to represent individual human souls in Russian belief, a widespread idea in other cultures, too.[2] There are other specific attributes given to stars in Russian lore: the appearance of a new star in the sky signifies the birth of a child, and the shooting star a death in the human world. A shooting star is in itself an ambivalent omen; in its potential for happiness, as well as bringing a wish, it can also be an indication of forthcoming marriage. Any unmarried girl who sees a shooting star should note the direction that it falls in, which will be the place to find her future husband. But, in a more sinister way, shooting stars are also feared as demons coming down to earth to seek out women for sexual intercourse; they have a particular fondness for ravishing virgins and recent widows. And even when a falling star is thought to embody the soul of an angel or an innocent child, this star can come to a bad end if it is captured by a witch, who places it in a sealed jar to languish there indefinitely. But whatever the significance of a falling star, the folk calendar decrees that it is best not to see one on March 5, as it will rob you instantly of your youth and beauty!

The connection between the birth of a child and the stars is also hallowed in an old birthing ritual. After the mother has given birth in the bathhouse, the midwife undresses herself, and walks naked around the outside of the bathhouse carrying the newborn child, who she presents to the Morning Star. This is said to help prevent the baby from crying in the early days of its life, but it is also a poetic rite that emphasizes the association between the new human soul and the starry regions from which it comes. Less poetic may be the effects of walking around without any clothes on in the Russian climate, so perhaps this custom has been confined to the summer season or to warmer southern climes (see Ryan 1999, p.52).

Wind and weather

One day, while on his way home, a peasant met three gentlemen coming towards him. The first, a chubby fellow, introduced himself to the peasant as the Sun, the second, who was grey-haired, thin and scrawny, announced that he was Frost, and the last character, who had tousled hair and puffed-up cheeks, said that his name was Wind. The peasant immediately bowed low to Mr Wind and ignored the other two. Frost and Sun were angered at his apparent lack of respect for them, and set about trying to punish him. But when the Sun shone fiercely upon him, fully intending to burn him up, his ally Wind cooled him with pleasant breezes, and when Frost turned everything around to winter, the peasant merely shrugged his shoulders, since Wind was ready to melt the ice with warm breezes. (From the story of *Sun, Frost, and Wind,* quoted in Warner 1985, p.48.)

This folktale is just one of many in Russia in which the elements are personified, and humans must reckon with their power, and take care not to offend them. Skill and wit may play a part, as they do here, when the peasant astutely recognizes the ultimate supremacy of Wind, thus ensuring his personal safety. But any attempt to dominate the elements usually meets with disaster, as it does in the story of Father Frost, where two girls are frozen to death in the forest for cheeking the mighty frost lord. In a climate of extreme seasons, where human life is always lived very close to the forces of nature, people have had to learn how to cope with the elements and to respect their power, if they wish to minimize the potential for disaster.

Whether or not Wind is always considered to be the strongest force, he is certainly paid due respect in Russian tradition. He may manifest as whirlwinds, which are characterized as wizards, dragons or demons; in the story of *The Three Kingdoms,* which we have already met, the Golden Kingdom is ruled by an angry and implacable whirlwind, which can only be conquered by trickery.

People were highly suspicious of whirlwinds, and if a strange, spiralling wind was seen to be whipping up dust or snow, any peasant passing by would plunge a knife into its centre to destroy the devil embodied there. Wind can also be allied with powers for good; he combines with St Lucian, the Christian saint, to form a character popularly known as Lukyan the Wind Wizard. Lukyan's day in the folk calendar is June 16, and is marked by a form of divination, in which peasants note how the wind blows in order to predict the kind of harvest they might expect. A southerly wind is an omen of a good harvest, whereas a northerly wind forecasts heavy rain for the rye fields in the autumn.

The sky region may be a world of its own, in the ancient three-tiered system, but it certainly influences the middle world of humans. The celestial bodies are considered to mingle with the elements and weather that exist closer to the earth, and in the Russian folk tradition, it is not really possible to draw a firm line between them. Weather, according to the traditional view, may be decreed by the spirits of the sky, and divination can be used as a magical means of penetrating this other world, and discovering what is in store.[3] There are a vast number of weather predictions in the folk tradition, both for the months of the year and the individual days. On February 2, for instance, a cloudy day means late snowstorms, on August 17, good weather signifies fair weather to come in November, and on December 12, a purple dawn may betoken cold winds for the rest of the month. General signs in everyday life can also be interpreted as weather omens, and birds can give notice of this, so that the cawing of a crow first thing in the morning has been thought to herald an imminent snowstorm, for instance.

Celestial portents

Although the practice of looking to the sky for omens is firmly embedded in the Russian native tradition, divination from the heavens by astrology is not a part of that tradition. It is entering Russian culture now, where astrology is a normal topic of conversation, and most people know not only their Western zodiac Sun sign, such as Gemini or Leo for instance, but their Chinese one, too — Rat, Horse, Dragon, and so on. But astrology, in terms of casting horoscopes, does not have any historical roots in Russia, unlike in the West, where this type of astrology goes back to the Middle Ages, introduced there from Arabic learning. Astrology began with the Babylonians, who patiently observed the movement of Sun, Moon and planets over hundreds of years, and from their findings were able to construct tables, which could ultimately be used to determine the precise position of the planets for any specific moment in time, past, present or future, an essential factor in drawing up a birth chart. Their knowledge passed to the Greeks, and finally to the Arabs, who introduced it into Western Europe.[4] Russia did not have direct access to this type of learning. As W.F. Ryan says: 'A lack of all but the most basic mathematics and the absence even of the concept of angular measurement ... made the development of mathematical astrology [in Russia] an impossibility' (Ryan 1999, p.373).

Russian sky divination is therefore based on phenomena that can be observed directly, but in this respect, it does have similarities with early astrology from Babylonian times. Both practices interpret the appearance of comets, and of visible lunar and solar phenomena, such as eclipses. In Russia, comets were traditionally seen as a harbinger of bloodshed, and eclipses as omens of disaster or divine wrath. As in Babylonian astrology, too, the Russian tradition observed the type of haloes that appeared around the Sun or Moon, and gave them specific meanings, based on their qualities, and the time that they appeared. An eighteenth century Russian manuscript declares: 'If the moon has a halo in June there will be war. If the moon has a halo in July there will be death to animals' (Ryan, p.134).

Perun, Lord of Thunder

It is, however, the spirits and deities who inhabit the Russian sky that loom largest, and the best example of these is that of Perun, lord of thunder. His reign dates from ancient times, and has carried on down through the ages, surviving the introduction of Christianity and lasting almost until the present day. The first recorded representation of Perun was at the end of the tenth century, when Vladimir I established his rule in Kiev, and honoured the prevailing gods by setting up statues to them in an official sanctuary. Perun, as the god of thunder and lightning, was revered as one of the greatest among them, and was fetchingly depicted with a silver head adorned with golden moustaches. The sanctuary was short-lived, however, since only eight years later, when Vladimir converted to Christianity, he had the statues thrown into the river in a fit of piety. Perun, the Slavic god, was officially no more. But he was not forgotten by the Russian people; the place where his statue became lodged downstream after the river had swept it away, was known thereafter as 'Perun's Bank'. The official command to depose Perun was likewise obeyed in the town of Novgorod, and his image there too was hurled from its position on the riverbank into the water, but the place has been revered right into modern times: 'Even in the twentieth century, the inhabitants of Novgorod were known to cast a coin into the river when passing the spot where Perun's image once stood' (Phillips & Kerrigan 1999, p.43). A current acknowledgment of the god of thunder includes a popular curse: 'May Perun take you!'

The Russian predilection for the practice of *dvoeverie,* or 'two faiths', keeping Christian and indigenous beliefs running in parallel, may have helped to save Perun from obscurity, for he speedily began an alliance with Elijah, the Old Testament prophet. Aspects of the two have merged over the course of time, and the association of Elijah with a primordial Slavic deity who sends down thunder and lightning, and punishes wrongdoers, is largely responsible for a fearful attitude to Elijah amongst Orthodox believers. Even in icons, Elijah is painted as a force to be reckoned with, rather than as a mystical sage. It is natural for Elijah to be closely associated with the sky because of his dramatic disappearance from the earth; as it says in the Bible: '... suddenly there appeared chariots of fire and horses of fire ... and Elijah was carried up in the whirlwind to heaven.' (2 Kings 2:11) He also declared: 'If I am a man of God, may fire fall from heaven and consume you and your company!' thus making him a premier choice in the popular imagination to pair up with the local god of thunder.

From this time on, Elijah and Perun could not easily be separated in Russian tradition. Elijah-Perun also held the unofficial title of Lord of the Harvest, and there was a need to court his approval in order to achieve good crops. August 2 is Elijah's feast day, on which everyone should rest from labour in his honour, and anyone daring to break that command is likely to be struck by thunderbolts sent by the prophet-god. He may also show his general displeasure towards disobedient peasants by setting fire to their hay, or flattening their crops with a shower of hailstones. However, like other Russian elemental spirits, he can also be benevolent, and holds the power to send much-needed rain to water the crops. 'Peasants imagined that he carried water on his chariot to all the saints in heaven, and when he spilled a little, life-giving moisture fell to earth. It was, therefore, to Elijah that they prayed for rain' (Ivanits 1992, p.30).

The merging of Perun with Elijah has been a fluid affair and he is also identified to a certain extent with other key figures from Christianity, such as St George, a very popular saint in Russia and patron of the city of Moscow, and the archangel Michael, both of whom are warriors and celestial forces who speed through the sky to defeat dragons or wrongdoers. Perun is also associated with John the Baptist, since on the feast day of St John at Midsummer, which is itself superimposed on an earlier solstice festival, 'Perun's flowers' may be found (see p.155). These magic, fire-like red flowers are said to bloom only on this one night of the year, and the hardy soul who not only discovers the flower, but can withstand the howling and assaults of jealous demons all night, will find treasure nearby in the morning (see Fig. 29).

All this might seem part of an old peasant tradition that has little to do with our own modern global concerns. However, not long ago, Perun's image turned up on the other side of the world, in an American evangelical website which drew on Russian mythology to prove that the devil had returned to earth in the form of President Putin, as an incarnation of Perun.

> The current Russian President, Putin by name, is a close prophetic match to the name 'Perun' described in the Russian Primary Chronicle. Since Putin came to office

> I have taken his family name as an indication that the Satan has returned to Russia, just as Revelation says he would. Putin is very likely the man who will actually call the world to war.[5]

At this writing, and although Putin is still in government, this prediction has not yet come true, and hopefully it never will.

Storms are traditionally seen as the medium through which Perun-Elijah reveals himself; in popular belief, a thunderclap is often explained as a sign that the god is driving his chariot across the sky. The thunderbolts that he hurls are believed to turn into stones popularly known as 'thunder arrows' (in actual fact fossils called belemnites), and these are revered as powerful talismans, once used by wizards in their magic, and which were buried with them in their graves. Although a fearful event, a thunderstorm can also be considered as sacred, and death by lightning as a form of blessing, ensuring that the soul of the deceased would go straight to heaven.[6] Nevertheless, few people actually want to be struck by lightning, and Russian country dwellers are afraid of thunderstorms, especially around the time of Elijah's feast day, the time when the saint-god is at work, striking down devils and evildoers. A stranger is not welcome at the house during a storm, since he might be one of these same devils on the run.

However powerful the celestial forces, though, humans can often find a way of dealing with them, as one folktale reveals. *The Peasant and the Saints* concerns a local farmer who preferred St Nicholas (the most popular Russian saint) to Elijah, and so decided to ignore Elijah's feast day and work in his fields as usual. Elijah, out for a stroll with Nicholas, noticed how splendidly the peasant's corn was growing as a result of his illicit labours, and swore to have his revenge. Nicholas is a soft-hearted saint, however, and he warned the peasant of Elijah's impending wrath, advising him to sell the crop immediately as it stood to the Church. Ignorant of the deal, Elijah blasted the corn with hailstorms, and was then mildly reproved by Nicholas, who told him that it was the Church which had suffered the loss. Elijah apologized for his haste, and restored the harvest in honour of the church, but not before Nicholas had passed on a tip to the peasant to buy the field back. Elijah was at first enraged by this trickery, but was finally appeased when the shrewd peasant lit a very large candle in his honour (Phillips & Kerrigan 1999, p.46).

Another tale begins with Perun, the Devil and a peasant sharing a hut in the forest, an uneasy situation that ends to the peasant's advantage when he manages to evict Perun and the Devil, simply by employing the tactic of keeping calm as Perun unleashes a thunderstorm around him, and the Devil a raging wind (from *The Carpenter, Perun & the Devil,* related in Phillips & Kerrigan, p.36). Although respect is shown in such stories for the power of the elements and the ancient gods or their Christian counterparts, there is a place for native cunning, and some inventive interaction between heaven and earth.

Journeys to the sky world

The sky world is the upper zone of the three-tiered Russian cosmos, and as these three zones are interconnected, it follows that humans can ascend into the upper world and have first-hand experience of it. We have already seen how this can come about, through the shaman's ascent to the spirit world, or as described in certain Russian folktales, such as the one of the old man who climbs up the cabbage stalk to reach the sky (see p.16). The individual human soul is also believed to journey to the sky after death. At one time, miniature ladders made of baked bread or knotted leather ropes were placed in coffins, to give the deceased some means of getting up there. The moon has sometimes been seen as the ultimate abode of dead souls, who have to find their way there as best they can, perhaps entering through the arch of the rainbow, or by treading the starry path of the Milky Way. This, however, is a hazardous route to take, as four giant mowers block the entry to the Milky Way, and will try to scythe down anyone attempting to pass through it to the heavenly regions.

Leaping horses, flying birds

The creatures in Russian mythology who play a special role mediating between sky and earth are horses and birds. It is easy to understand why birds are seen as sky messengers, and why they have long represented happiness in Russian folklore, soaring upwards as they do towards the heavens, and symbolizing the flight of the human soul to those regions. The horse may be less obvious as a sky spirit, but its ability to leap high puts it in the realm of supernatural celestial beings, and tales of winged horses also grant it the powers of flight. In the Siberian story related above, of *The Sun Maiden and the Crescent Moon,* the Sun Maiden summons a winged horse by striking the heavens with her head, and she gives this horse to her lover to help him return to earth. Perhaps the sky horse is vulnerable when he leaves the celestial world, for he is attacked by an evil sorceress on earth, who tears off one of his hind legs, thus reducing his power.

Horses are strongly associated with the Sun in Russian symbolism, and they are often carved onto ridge poles and the gable end of traditional Russian houses, signifying the link between sky spirits and the upper portion of the home, as mentioned in Chapter 3, p.58. They may also appear alongside the image of the Mother Goddess; as already described in Chapter 2, she may be represented as a triangular female figure, standing on the back of a horse. It is thought that this may be an indication that she is not just confined to earth, but that her fecundity is found in the higher world too, and sky spirits thus serve her as the mother of all creation.

The best-known magical horse in Russian folklore is *Sivka-Burka.* In the story of the same name, this magnificent steed issues forth from the grave of a *bogatyr* hero at midnight. It is commanded to arise by the spirit of the *bogatyr,* who then awards it as a prize to his youngest son, Ivan, now keeping vigil by his father's grave, a task that his elder brothers were too lazy or scared to perform. As the horse springs to life, the earth trembles, sparks of fire fly from his eyes, and hot steam bursts from his nostrils.

Ivan and Sivka-Burka make their alliance, and the lad learns to call up the horse from underground every time he needs him, and how to bid him to jump high. This connects Sivka-Burka, the magical leaping horse, firmly to the older shamanic tradition, where the horse is associated with the flight of the shaman up into the sky world. A horse may be the spirit medium or guide which the shaman encounters in trance, and which will convey him to the upper regions. Often shamans drum and dance to imitate a galloping horse, conjuring up the energy for the ascent, and sometimes in days gone by, a real horse was sacrificed before the shamanic journey was taken. In *Sivka-Burka,* the horse leaps up as high as the castle battlements with Ivan on his back, allowing the young man to snatch the ring out of the hand of the beautiful princess who is waiting there; she has promised to marry the first man who can achieve this. After the story resolves with the happy union of the couple, Sivka-Burka disappears, never to be seen again. He is a spirit who has helped a human being to rise from the underworld to the heights, and like many a magical helper, he is there when he is needed and returns to his own realms after the task is done.

It is worth mentioning that in this fairy story, as in many Russian tales, success comes to the youngest brother, the one who is normally at the end of the line for attention, prestige and inheritance. Not uncommonly, as in this case, he is also considered as the ugliest and the most stupid of the brothers. The father often retains a special fondness for his clumsy or suppressed youngest son, however, and it usually turns out that the awkward lad is transformed into a handsome, intelligent suitor at the end of the story. In the tale of *Sivka-Burka,* this happens after Ivan wins the contest and the Princess has accepted him for her own. She honours her pledge, even though it seems that she will have to marry a ragged simpleton. Then Ivan changes before her eyes into a richly-dressed, good-looking prince, and the wedding takes place with great joy.

There is something of the Fool about Ivan, and other similar heroes of Russian fairy tales. (Ivan is the commonest name for the hero too, corresponding to Jack or John in the British tradition. Vasilisa is the name most commonly used for Russian heroines.) But their folly is only in the common eyes of the world, for they are usually loyal, affectionate, observant and persistent. The truth shines through them, and magical creatures are willing to serve them.

Firebird

> It was the Firebird. Prince Ivan opened his eyes with a start, alerted by her shining magnificence, as she perched in the tree above him. He reached out his hand to grasp

> her, but she was too quick for him, and launched herself into flight. As her wings opened, they filled the orchard with a blaze of light, so dazzling that he could no longer even see the golden apples upon which she had been feasting. Night had been banished by her. With one last desperate effort, he reached up as high as he could, and seized her tail. One feather came away in his hand, and then the Firebird was gone.
>
> This feather that he held was all that remained of her glory. But what a glory that was — its brilliant light shone throughout the palace. Prince Ivan could not rest; it was as though he himself was on fire. A longing for the quest had taken hold of him. He would seek her; he would leave the Palace to follow the Firebird. (From the story of *Prince Ivan and the Firebird:* Author's re-telling.)

The Firebird is the bird of light and inspiration in Russian legend (see Fig.1). She flies to and fro over the land, and every now and then a feather drops from her tail. Where it falls, according to popular belief, a new artistic tradition will spring up.[7] Or it may be the beginning of a new fairy story, triggered when the hero discovers the shining feather and goes in search of the Firebird. *Zharptitsa,* the Russian word for Firebird, is always feminine. Perhaps this is because the name itself, built on the word for bird, *ptitsa,* is feminine in gender, but in any case, like a beautiful and elusive woman, she can stir up envy and greed as well as more honourable aspirations. In the story of *The Firebird and Princess Vasilisa,* a huntsman who comes across a golden feather of the Firebird, shining bright as a flame, lives to regret presenting it to his king as a gift. The king is inflamed with desire, and demands that the huntsman should also bring him the Firebird herself, on pain of his life. This the huntsman does, but his success is followed by a further demand to find and bring back Princess Vasilisa, so that the King may marry her. Princess Vasilisa lives at the edge of the world, where the red Sun rises, and it takes some time and a number of testing adventures before the huntsman's persistence is rewarded. Dutiful to the king's command up until now, he finally manages to turn the tables, surviving an ordeal by boiling water, in which the king perishes, and is able to claim Princess Vasilisa for himself.

The story of *Prince Ivan and the Firebird* is also a quest, but one in which young Prince Ivan sets off on the trail of the Firebird after he has discovered her stealing the golden apples in his father's orchard at night. Her blaze of light in the night-time orchard distinguishes her as a mythic bird of the sky realm. It is a beautifully woven story, in which Grey Wolf is the other chief character, playing the part of a trickster spirit. He appears at first to threaten the young prince by eating his horse, but becomes his most loyal helper, guiding the prince through various misadventures. When the prince catches up with the Firebird, he finds her kept in a golden cage, hung in a garden filled with a wonderful light. Grey Wolf advises Prince Ivan simply to take the Firebird and leave her cage behind, but he seizes her finely-wrought cage as well. This sets off a terrible jangling noise, as the cage is strung with invisible wires attached to all the trees in the garden, which are hung with bells that ring as an alarm. Guards seize him, and he is brought before the king of that place, who agrees to spare his life only on condition that Ivan fetches him the Horse with the Golden Mane and Tail.

So it goes on; Grey Wolf advises, and Ivan ignores his advice. The Prince is thus precipitated from one sticky situation to another until finally, just when he is on the brink of success, riding home with the Firebird, the Horse with the Golden Mane and Tail, and the lovely Princess Vasilisa as well, he is set upon by his jealous brothers, who hack him to pieces and take the prizes back to the palace for themselves. Once again, Grey Wolf rescues Ivan, by sending a raven to fetch the Waters of Life and Death from the Otherworld to heal his dismembered body. Finally, Ivan is restored to life, and reaches home just in time to denounce his evil brothers and marry the Princess himself.

This story is redolent with symbolism and can be read in different ways, from a fairy tale rich with imagery and adventure, to a pilgrimage of the human soul. The quest is initiated by the appearance of the Firebird, like a revelation, a blaze of light which is a sign of another world beyond our own. The feather is a reminder of this, some spark of inspiration that has come into the human soul, which lodges there, and which urges us to go forward and follow the path. A crossroads can mark the way, giving us a hard time in making what seem impossible choices. In Ivan's case, he comes to a milestone which declares:

Straight ahead lies hunger and cold.
To the right — life and health to you, but death to your horse.
To the left — death to you, but life and health to your horse.

Trials and tests of courage and purpose arise. But the creature who seems to be our greatest enemy, like Grey Wolf, can actually turn out to be our most faithful helper. Fear and preconceptions have to be stripped away so that we can embrace a new purpose, and accept a new reality. It is also a very human story, for although the hero Ivan defies the good advice that Grey Wolf gives him, the wolf does not lose patience with him. Life forces are ultimately benevolent, and if we are true to our destiny, the path will stay open before us, even if it twists and turns along the way.[8] Ivan's folly leads him into further adventures, but these are also the key to his transformation; without being captured by the guards, for instance, he would never have gone further to find the Horse with the Golden Mane and Tail, or the Princess Vasilisa. His journey takes him into the realm of death itself, a loss of self corresponding to a stage that inevitably comes at some point in the path of spiritual transformation. In Christianity, it is known as the Dark Night of the Soul, and in alchemy as the Nigredo, or Blackening. But when his own powers are spent, help comes from a higher source, in this case in the form of his faithful friend Grey Wolf, who procures the Waters of Life and Death from the world beyond. After Ivan has sacrificed everything, including his own life, all is restored to him, and he returns to the place he came from, enriched beyond measure. The journey leads back to the starting point, but all is changed.

The story can thus be read as one of human transformation and enlightenment, which is literally triggered by the brilliant light of the Firebird. There are episodes in it which can be read at a profound level, such as the one where Prince Ivan captures the Firebird in her cage. He is warned to leave the trappings behind, and take only the Firebird herself. This is similar to the experience of meditation, where the heart of the meditative experience is to go beyond images and thoughts, and the meditator's instructions are to let them go, however attractive and tempting they may be. Seizing the beautiful cage is like taking possession of these fine and inspiring thoughts, but when the meditator does so, then the alarm bells ring, the jangling of everyday consciousness returns, and the deep, peaceful contemplative state recedes.

Fairy stories can thus be a source of wisdom, capable of being read at different levels. Not all lend themselves to such a degree of in-depth reflection as this one does, but the best among them can be seen as real parables of transformation. They can touch on the mysteries of life and death, and on the changes of state that humans can attain. In terms of the Firebird, although she is unique to Russia in the form that she appears, she is a manifestation of what may be a universal symbol. There are many similar images to the Firebird, both in the literature of spirituality and in folktales from other cultures. Consciousness is described as golden light in the Chinese treatise on meditation, *The Secret of the Golden Flower,* for instance. The divine bird of fire or light is recorded in various cultures; it is known as the sacred Simurgh in Central Asian myth, and similar golden birds turn up in stories recorded across a wide stretch of countries from Ireland to Africa. There is even a folklorist's term for the genre of such stories as *Prince Ivan and the Firebird,* known as 'The Quest for the Golden Bird'.

Birds of happiness, birds as messengers and husbands

Birds are a symbol of happiness in Russian culture. They are commonly painted on Matrioshka nesting dolls, often in the form of hens, to bring happiness to the owner, and, since drinking was also presumed to be a joyous activity, early drinking vessels were often made in the shape of a bird. Using the form of a bird to contain drink, food or sweetmeats has survived right until the present era in folk art. In Khokhloma design a duck or a swan is sometimes carved from wood, painted and lacquered in a striking combination of black, red and gold, and little drinking cups are hooked onto its side, ready to be dipped into the liquid that will fill the hollow of the bird. One can also acquire, as I have, neatly carved and polished wooden birds which have little hollows in their back just right for holding sweets or salt or nuts.

Specific birds may also have the meaning of happiness; the crane is associated with the joy of summer's return, as well as with feminine grace. To witness a flock of cranes in a Russian meadow, each standing delicately poised, as I have done, is a truly miraculous sight, bringing a sense of the sublime. The favourite bird of winter, too, the *snegir* or Russian bullfinch, is loved for its warm colouring, for its deep red breast, and for being seen as a flash of life and beauty among the frosty trees. There are also mythical birds of happiness or paradise in Russian culture, the best known of which are the Sirin, and Alkonost, although these can also be portrayed as happiness and sorrow respectively. They are thought to have come originally from Greek myth, and are not, strictly speaking, a part of the Slavic tradition. But once the concept of bird as heavenly messenger and bringer of good fortune was established in early Russian tradition, it is possible that imported legends were readily adapted into this form.

As active spirits, however, birds are more commonly depicted as messengers. In the story of *Prince Ivan and the Firebird,* the raven acts as a messenger and courier between this world and the Otherworld, designated as it is also in other Russian fairy stories as 'the thrice tenth kingdom, beyond the thrice ninth land'. Bird as messenger is a universally common motif, but the role of the raven here may have an ancient connection with the two ravens Hugin and Mugin in Norse mythology, who are known as 'thought' and 'memory' respectively. These birds are spies of the god Odin; each day they travel round the world, and at night they return to the realm of the gods to perch on Odin's shoulders, and whisper the day's news into his ears. The raven also plays a significant part in Siberian shamanism, where the bird is 'the shaman's faithful and favourite informant.' Here, too, the shaman may have two raven spirits sitting one on each shoulder (see Kenin-Lopsan, Boraxoo & Taylor 1997).

Because birds can travel between two worlds, their calls and songs are considered to be significant, indicative of what is happening elsewhere, or what is to come. Tuvan Siberians, for instance, fear the death of a child when the horned owl cries near the settlement, and forecast weather from the call of the black woodpecker. Similarly, Russian peasants would listen to the call of the rook on March 17 to divine the quality of the weather and the harvests for that year. A charming fairy story, *The Lad Who Knew the Language of the Birds,* tells how a young lad called Vassily finds he can understand the song of a nightingale that is kept as a caged bird. The nightingale becomes his companion; they travel together, and the nightingale predicts the future, warns of forthcoming storms and finally interprets the calling of ravens who are troubling a king to the monarch's satisfaction — so much so, that he gives his daughter to Vassily in marriage (Afanasiev 1983, *Words of Wisdom,* p.76).

The idea that human beings can understand the language of the birds is still retained in Russian folk memory; it is not exclusive to Russia, of course, and may be a universal belief retained from the animistic and shamanic religions, indicating that we, as humans, are a part of the living cosmos, and that by opening ourselves to this teeming sphere of life, we can to some extent dissolve the boundaries of our own individual identity, and align ourselves with other forms of life, understanding their language and their innate wisdom. It is the foundation of the shamanic trance state, and seems to arise spontaneously even in our more 'rational' modern Western society. A friend of mine once told me how she had experienced the sensation of being a fox, of becoming that creature completely, and being able to look through its eyes. Antonia White also wrote about it in her semi-autobiographical novel, *Beyond the Glass,* a remarkable work describing how the heroine Clara descends into the underworld of insanity and emerges again. She suffers visions (for these are not necessarily pleasant experiences) in which she lives and dies as a salmon, as a horse, and finally, with 'skull split like a shell', is 'born and re-born with incredible swiftness as a woman, as an imp, as a dog, and finally as a flower', returning at last to human consciousness.[9]

The shaman may to some extent merge with a bird as he practises his vision trance; the shaman Herel, who I visited in Tuva in

Siberia, wore a headdress made of eagle feathers, which may have been a way of helping him to connect with the bird spirit which enables him to fly to the sky world. This spirit is known in one Siberian tradition as Markut, Bird of Heaven. As the session with Herel proceeded, I sat on a bearskin rug with my eyes closed as he danced, drummed, and chanted around me. My consciousness settled down from initial fear and tearfulness to a still and luminous state, and while in that phase, I saw with my inner eye an eagle sitting by my side, a calm, intelligent, but ethereal presence. At that time, I had no idea that there was any eagle symbolism involved, as Herel had donned his eagle feather headdress after I shut my eyes; my travelling companion, Lyn, who sat quietly by and witnessed the session, later gave me a faithful account of what happened. It is likely that the eagle in this case represented the shaman's personal spirit helper, which can take different animal or bird forms, but Herel, like a good shaman, kept its identity secret and would not tell us what type of guide he had (see Fig. 8).[10]

Some Russian fairy stories may contain a cross-over between early shamanism and traditional belief, since they depict birds that are half human. There are several tales in which birds become husbands to human girls, such as that of *Maria Morevna,* the Warrior Queen, who we shall meet in the next chapter; her husband has three sisters, all of whom have married birds — a falcon, eagle and raven — and which can all change appearance between a bird and a handsome young man. One of the best known tales of bird husbands is that of *Fenist, the Bright Falcon,* a tender and touching story about a young girl who asks her father for the gift of a feather from Fenist. When she receives it through the good offices of a stranger, she is able to summon up Fenist the Falcon in person, and they marry and enjoy great happiness together. By day, he flies in the sky as a falcon, and at night he visits Maria in the form of a handsome youth. But her sisters are jealous, and they plot to harm Fenist by sticking knives on the window frame through which he enters; wounded and bleeding, the bird flies away, calling to his bride that she will only ever find him again in that magical realm beyond the thrice-nine land, in the thrice tenth kingdom. Maria sets off bravely in search of him; as predicted, she does not find him until she has 'worn out three pairs of iron shoes, broken three iron staffs, and eaten three stone loaves', all of which take her through fearsome encounters and adventures. Eventually, she succeeds; the couple are united again, and love and bravery are rewarded.

I had my own particular experience of a strange encounter with a bird in Russia in the winter of 2001, when I was writing the last chapters for a book on alchemy, with the theme of personal transformation, and the making of gold in the human soul. I was staying on the sixteenth floor of a bleak tower block hotel in a suburb of Moscow and was just thinking about a Gnostic text in which an eagle appears as a sacred messenger, when I suddenly became aware that a bird had flown in through my own window. It was a blue tit, a *sinitsa* or 'little bluebird', as it is known in Russian. Birds were few and far between in the city at this time of year, which was gripped by an icy spell and besides, my window was open only a crack, and covered by lace curtains. I had no idea how it had managed to fly up so high, and to get inside; luckily, I was soon able to release it again.

Just after this, I went out to do some shopping in the local market, and on return, tipped out the contents of my bag onto the bed. A gold ring tumbled out from the bottom of the bag. I had no idea where it might have come from, I could not trace the owner, and I have it still; bird and gold, message and symbol, seem mysteriously, and wonderfully allied in this extraordinary episode. (See Gilchrist 2002, pp.162–3.) It was not, in one sense, specifically an event from the Russian tradition, but was perhaps an example of the kind of magical dialogue that seems to take place between 'heaven and earth' at certain times, wherever we might find ourselves, and which may, as it were, tap into local resources, and become embodied in these. Certainly, the blue tit with its meaning of 'bluebird' in Russian, and the connotations relating to 'the bluebird of happiness' in Western culture, make it a remarkably appropriate choice to represent alchemical transformation in the form of a bird.[11]

The sky is part of an animate cosmos in the Russian tradition, as we have seen, and perhaps this is not just the stuff of fairy stories, but real and valid human experience, as recent philosophical and cultural studies are now pointing out.[12] To contemplate this, we have to attune ourselves to a worldview in which everything in this sky is connected and part of a greater being — the Sun, Moon and stars, the birds flying through the air, and the weather that comes and goes. Everything has its own force and spirit. Seen in this light, inherited folklore beliefs are not just quaint traditions, but part of an active engagement between humans and the 'otherworld', a celestial drama fearsome in its scale and awesome in power.

5

The Secrets of Life and Death

Baba Yaga and the Borderlands

> Beyond the thrice-nine lands, in the thrice-ten kingdom there lives Baba-Yaga, the witch. Her house stands in a forest beyond the Flaming River. (*Maria Morevna*)

Baba Yaga is an ugly, cantankerous old woman, who lives in a hut that stands on chicken's feet in the middle of the forest, and who flies around the skies by means of a pestle and mortar. She captures small children, tricks young maidens, and kills just about anyone who crosses her. This wicked witch of Russian fairy stories is familiar to every person in the land, and her fame, or notoriety, has spread further afield, so that she is also well-known in Europe and America. She is a stock character in folktales, and also turns up regularly in other contexts, in modern Russian cartoons and children's books, as a puppet, and in more high-minded art as a character in Modest Mussorgsky's suite of music, *Pictures from an Exhibition.*[1] Baba Yaga is also a useful weapon for Russian parents to use, as a way of frightening small children who are misbehaving.

'Sit down, and finish your supper, otherwise Baba Yaga will come for you.'

Olga, otherwise an extremely patient grandmother, had finally had enough of small Dima's noisy behaviour at the supper table. On hearing the dreaded name, he subsided instantly, a watchful, fearful look in his eyes as he sat back quietly to eat his meal. A few minutes later, though, after the threat of the witch had worn off, he began to jump up and down again.

Olga was quick to react. She got to her feet and peered out of the window.

'Baba Yaga's coming down the lane now,' she said.

Dima was back in his seat before any of us could blink twice, and we finished our evening meal in peace. Baba Yaga is fond of stealing little children in order to cook them up for her own supper.

But although she has a worldwide reputation, and is a star of wonder tales, woodcuts, comics and animated films, she remains enigmatic and ambivalent, ultimately a mysterious figure whose source is unknown. No one is quite sure of her origins, her function, or even of whether she is ultimately a force for good or evil.[2] All studies seem to agree, however, that her role is much more than that of a pantomime-style witch. Baba Yaga stands at the boundaries of life and death, and it is this border country of life and death, darkness and rebirth, which we will be exploring in this chapter. It is a terrain inhabited also by Koshchei the Deathless, and Mishka the bear, as well as by wolf-wizards and witches in human society.

'Leg of stone, toothless crone'

Baba Yaga is of grotesque appearance, with lank greasy hair, a long nose, and a leg which may either be made of stone in polite renderings, or of faeces in more earthy accounts. Her bulk fills up her hut when she is at home, and, when out of it, she flies around in a mortar made of iron, which she steers with a pestle. Sometimes, as in the story mentioned below, she rides instead on a magic horse chosen from her herd of doughty mares. She lives deep in the forest, and has a fondness for killing and perhaps eating visitors, whose skulls she nails to posts impaled in the ground around her hut. This hut also has the property of revolving at the witch's command, hiding or concealing its entrance according to her word.

In common parlance, the term Baba Yaga is used in Russian for any cantankerous old woman. There is no common agreement as to where the Yaga (or Iaga, Ega, Egibihk and other variations) part of her name comes from. The 'Baba' prefix refers to woman or mother, but Yaga may be connected to the word for snake, for pain, or even for pelican, according to various authorities, or, more likely, to none of these.

Her role in traditional stories is to challenge anyone who strays into her domain, whom she may then attack, kill, advise, help or strike a bargain with, or perform a combination of these functions. She is fond of Russian blood, in terms of drinking or spilling it, and can smell it approaching from afar. New arrivals are often greeted with the question: 'Are you here to do something, or are you running away from something?' — words that suggest a ritual confrontation, a challenge to test the visitor's determination. Her attitude towards children and girls is different to the stance she takes with young men, since she may capture and consume small children, she may imprison young girls or choose to let them go unharmed, but she always challenges and tests youths and men. This has led to a theory that Baba Yaga is in origin the ancient goddess of the underworld, who conducts young men through initiation ceremonies at their coming of age. They must show bravery and cunning, avoid the traps and snares that she sets, and perform near-impossible tasks in order to win through and be worthy of manhood.

In the story of Maria Morevna, quoted at the opening of the chapter, Prince Ivan encounters Baba Yaga when he is in search of his abducted wife, the warrior queen Maria Morevna. Baba Yaga's house is surrounded by twelve poles, all but one crowned with a human head, and Ivan recognizes that the last one has been saved for his own head to crown. But Baba Yaga promises to spare him, and grant him his freedom, if he will look after her horses for three days. She has many fine mares, and flies around the world each day on one of them; she is ready to offer Ivan one of these magical steeds if he can care for the whole herd.

The task is more difficult than he thinks, since for two days running, the horses gallop off into the forest as soon as he gets them out to pasture, and he falls into a heavy slumber till the end of the day. But he is then helped by creatures that he has been kind to earlier in his travels, and manages to get the herd back to the house with the mares intact. At midnight, knowing that Baba Yaga will never honour her promise, he decides to escape; he steals a colt and rides off towards the flaming river, where his wife waits for him on the other side.

Going to sleep on the job, as we saw with the story of *Prince Ivan and the Firebird,* is a mistake for young would-be heroes, and in this case it may correspond with the sleep deprivation that often accompanies initiation rites, where keeping a vigil can form a significant phase in the process. All the old habits of eating, sleeping and bathing must be uprooted, and Baba Yaga's offer of steam baths and food in some stories may be echoes of new and possibly dangerous experiences in this department. Some authorities have objected to the notion of Baba Yaga as an initiator of young men, as she is female, but there is a strong tradition of women initiating boys into manhood in various societies, for instance in Western Europe in the early Middle Ages, when women would give young men their weapons so that they could become warriors or knights. This has historical foundation, and, in mythology, King Arthur himself is said to have received his magical sword Excalibur from the Lady of the Lake. It also makes sense in terms of magical polarity, and of energy exchanged between male and female, that one sex initiates another. A female deity may commonly have male acolytes too, as in the ancient Phrygian cult of the goddess Cybele.

Male initiation is often sexual, too. The horrific appearance of Baba Yaga as an ugly old crone, who may also be farting and exposing her foaming genitalia, denotes the reverse of everything lovely and maidenly. This may challenge the young man's unquestioning attachment to the beauty of the female form, and force him to look with different eyes at an adult woman. The witch is also the opposite of the comforting, familiar mother figure, and this may help to break his dependence upon his mother in order to claim his manhood, and allow him to make a new and truer bond with a woman who can become his wife. In the story of Maria Morevna, although Ivan is married to her already, she is abducted on account of his naivety and carelessness, as we shall see shortly, and it is only by showing genuine bravery and effort that he can finally reclaim her, and make her truly his own.

If the forest ritual was once a cultural event, marking the passage from youth into manhood, then most likely it would have been enacted by a person, male or female, dressed up as Baba Yaga, and probably masked to give a terrifying appearance. Some weight is lent to this by the fact that fairy stories may contain 'a' Baba Yaga, or even several of them, suggesting that there could be local Baba Yagas. There may be three sister Baba Yagas, for instance. This may also relate to the symbolism of the triple goddess, an idea which is widespread through various cultures. The three faces or figures of this goddess are maiden, mother and crone, and there is no doubt that in this schema, Baba Yaga would be a manifestation of the crone figure. It is also common for each of the three archetypes to be divided into a further triplicity, giving three sets of three and ultimately a circle of nine goddesses.[3] Thus we would have the three sister crones or Baba Yagas, each one slightly differentiated perhaps, and related to the three maidens and three mothers within the group as a whole.

The symbolism of the triple goddess is intimately connected with the phases of the moon, so that the maiden can be seen as the crescent moon, who then grows to fullness as mother, and finally declines into the dark phase as the crone, a phase associated with Hecate in Greek myth, for instance. The crone may be frightening, old, smelly and in some ways evil, but she is also the embodiment of wisdom, and no understanding of woman is complete without her. It has also been suggested that Baba Yaga's hut, which revolves to conceal or reveal its opening, may itself be associated with cycles of the moon, and of feminine sexuality, so that Baba Yaga's role as crone could also thus embody knowledge about female sexual cycles, about menstruation and the waxing and waning of fertility and desire, knowledge which young men need to acquire as they are about to enter into relationships with the opposite sex. Such an interpretation also goes a long way to explaining the ambivalence of Baba Yaga, and how she can never be finally upheld as totally good or evil.

The much-loved tale of *Vasilisa the Fair* gives us a heroine's perspective on an encounter with Baba Yaga. Young Vasilisa is sent to the forest by her cruel stepsisters to fetch a light from Baba Yaga's house in the forest. On approaching the hut, she meets three horsemen, one white, one scarlet and one black; they represent Day, Sun and Night, and they are under Baba Yaga's command, for she, as many stories about her relate, has power over the winds and weather, Sun and Moon. Baba Yaga sniffs out

Vasilisa's approach, and offers her a light only on condition that the little girl stays and works for her. The tasks seem impossible, but Vasilisa has an ally — a little magic doll that her mother gave to her as she lay dying. The doll helps her to do the housework, and finally Baba Yaga turns Vasilisa out of the house and gives her the light she requested to take home.

In terms of the lunar cycles and the symbolism of the triple goddess, Vasilisa may be seen as the 'maiden' phase of the moon, and her mother as the full moon, who died then to be followed by the black lunar crone. Vasilisa wins the light of her crescent moon back by braving Baba Yaga's darkness, and earning her respect through hard work and integrity. Perhaps Baba Yaga once played a part in coming of age ceremonies for young girls too, but I have not come across any mention of this.

Baba Yaga is a figure who stands at the borders of life and death, and as both boys and girls have to die to their childhood in order to enter the adult world, she is an appropriate figure to meet them on the threshold of that transition. She is herself a symbol of death in some old folklore customs; at harvest time, for instance, an effigy of Baba Yaga may be created in straw, and subsequently destroyed. This is said to act as a reminder that the day of reaping and death comes to us all.

In many tales, it is made clear that the witch lives close to the borders of the otherworld. One hero finds her abode right at the end of the earth: 'A little hut stood there, with no road beyond it, but only darkness so deep that the eye could not pierce it,' as we are told in the story of *The Enchanted Princess.* Baba Yaga's territory is already considered to be in the world of 'the living dead', known as the 'thrice-nine land '. This lies far beyond the human realm, and from here one must set out to confront the final boundary to the 'thrice-ten kingdom', often understood as the realm of the truly dead. This boundary may be described as the 'flaming river' (as above), or 'the blue sea'. In one story, it is charmingly defined as the 'Currant River', crossed by the 'Cranberry Bridge'. Indeed, it is not enough just to reach the boundary, for a means must be found or created to pass over it. In the story of *Maria Morevna,* Ivan calls up a bridge by waving a magic kerchief, a trick often employed to make it passable. In fairy stories such as this, the hero is usually able to perform the superhuman feat of going to the 'thrice-ten land' and returning, perhaps as young men once did symbolically through their ritual ordeals.

Whatever the final definition of Baba Yaga, if such a thing is possible, she remains as a figure who can both attract us to the darkness of her mysteries and repel us with her disgusting appearance and unpleasant ways. She also remains a key archetype in Russian mythology, represented not only in stories but in popular rhymes, and in old folk woodcuts, known as *lubok*. In one famous and often copied *lubok*, she is depicted as fighting something described as a 'crocodile', but which looks more like a furry figure, or a bearded man with a tail (see Fig. 12). This has been interpreted as representing a political satire on Catherine the Great (the witch) fighting with Peter the Great (the foreigner, and thus the exotic, non-Russian and dangerous crocodile). However, one study goes to great lengths to show that this is not so, and that we are still in the realm of myth with this image. It points out that both Baba Yaga and the crocodile are designated as guardians of the underworld in traditional lore, implying a magical theme; it suggests that the appearance of the so-called crocodile as half human, half furry animal may in fact indicate that this is a shaman magician (see Farrell 1993, pp. 725–44). These magicians, or wizards, were real life characters who grew their hair and beards long, but they were popularly regarded as a combination of beast and man. According to recorded accounts given by the wizards themselves, there were also battles traditionally fought between witches and sorcerers, and it may be one of these old magical battles that is depicted here, albeit in a light-hearted manner.

Wolf wizards, psychics and healers

Wizards were once part of a mighty class of sorcerers in Russia, whose powers were both coveted and feared. Although these were probably predominantly men, women were known to take part as well, and eventually, as their status declined, the men became local wizards practising in village communities, offering rituals to mark rites of passage and to avert ill fortune, and their female counterparts became known as wise women, *znaharki*, who could provide magical charms and old remedies to heal. But up until at least the early eighteenth century, sorcerers were found practising in all ranks of society and there were high profile cases where those who had offended royalty or nobility were executed, even in one instance on the order of Peter the Great himself (Farrell 1993, p.738).

Education and class does not diminish the love of magic and mysterious powers in Russia, powers which may also provoke an antagonistic response, but are never completely denied. Perhaps this is why the monk Rasputin, with his reputation for miracle cures and hypnotic charm, gained such power over the wife and the court of the last Tsar of Russia. It may also be why psychic powers were the subject of serious research by the Soviet Government, and individuals today who appear to possess out-of-the-ordinary abilities to heal rapidly become well-known throughout the country.

There are many forms of alternative and psychic healing in the West, too, plus clairvoyants who can be consulted for prediction and for receiving messages from the spirit world. But these are in most cases set well apart from conventional medical or scientific establishments, and are considered to be unorthodox at best, and downright dangerous at worst. Many of us as individuals may have had psychic or telepathic experiences, and we may take an interest in astrology or perhaps have sensed the presence of beings from other worlds entering our lives on occasion. But such experiences are usually kept to oneself, or revealed only to others who share such an interest, in case they will be mocked at by society.[4] In Russia, this does not seem to be so, and there is room for experimental treatments that may defy current laws of science, and for the public acknowledgment of healers who appear to possess extraordinary powers.

One example is that of the former circus performer, Dikul, who now has his own well-known rehabilitation centre in Moscow for treating patients with spinal injuries, and which was formerly sponsored by the Soviet government. Dikul suffered an accident while working in the circus, and broke his back, leaving him paralysed. By his own efforts, he apparently managed to retrain his muscles to move and so walk again, and has restored the damaged nerves, even though according to conventional medical science, this should not be possible. And although Dr Dikul gives a kind of scientific explanation for how this works (due to an inbuilt capacity, he says, for spinal cord cells to heal themselves), much of his treatment depends on the will and belief of the patient. It is not a laying-on of hands, and the patient must work hard in physical terms, but much is due to faith, and putting mind over matter. As Dikul says:

> I can tell you how to do things, but without your will my words will not bring success. Even if my equipment was made of gold, you will never walk if you do not believe you can. You will have to work with the same devotion, discipline and will power every day for many years, if needed. Only then you will be able to say: '*I have done it, I can walk*'.[5]

Perhaps this belief in breakthroughs, in miracles even, is an indication of the readiness in Russia to accept greater truths than the rational mind can encompass. As Fedor Tiutchev, the nineteenth century poet, expressed it, Russia is a unique case:

Russia cannot be understood with the mind alone,
No ordinary yardstick can measure her greatness:
She stands alone, unique —
In Russia one can only believe.

In 1999, when I was organizing an exhibition of Russian lacquer miniatures in the UK, Pyotr Mityashin, the artist who was coming from Russia as my chief demonstrator, was in a terrible road accident about ten days before the show was due to open. He suffered a fractured skull and broken vertebrae, and lay in a coma for several weeks. Although he eventually recovered in all other ways, he remained paralysed as a result. The show had to go on without an artist, but all of us were desperately concerned for him and in the early stages, still full of hope that he might walk again.

Sasha, a practical but sensitive man who acted as my driver when I visited Moscow, had met Pyotr and felt a warm friendship towards him, and consulted a psychic on his behalf to see what might come about.

'I trust this person absolutely,' Sasha said. 'And she says he will walk again — not as well as before, and he will wear special kind of boots to do so. But he *will* walk.'

In one sense, the clairvoyant was right. For various reasons, Pyotr did not go to the Dikul centre, but instead a fund was organized by well-wishers to provide rehabilitation in the UK. The doctors at the specialist unit told us that there was virtually no chance that our artist friend would walk naturally again — but they did recommend that he should use some callipers, comprising full length leg braces, and with the aid of crutches and the strong use of his upper body, Pyotr was able to swing himself around for short distances. This shows up one of the pitfalls of clairvoyance, that the image perceived was accurate, but the interpretation was not. All psychic impressions come through a human filter, and they are subject to our own human suggestibility; this is not to say that they are based on fantasy, or are useless, only that we must take care in interpreting them, and not expect one hundred percent accuracy.

The tradition of wizardry in Russia probably continued in a diversity of forms after the religion of shamanism was officially left behind, making it hard to define one main practice of magic. Names used for sorcerers were also diverse, especially if the concept is taken to include witches, healers and fortune-tellers. *Koldun* came to be used as the name for a village wizard, with *kudesnik* employed as another well-known term, but there were also the words such as *charovnik* (spell-caster), *ved'ma* (a knower and usually a female sorcerer), and the ancient term *volkhv,* which has given rise to the modern adjective *volshebni,* 'magical'. To my knowledge, no study has entirely concentrated on this topic of wizardry, and so although there are many allusions in writings past and present to the doings of wizards, there is no real sense of how the tradition operated as a whole. The coming of Christianity also blurred matters, as it brought in the concept of the devil, and to some extent polarized wizardry and witchcraft against the official religion, so that sorcerers and witches then came to be associated with devils and black magic. These were different concepts to those first inherited from shamanism, in which shamans might in particular cases use their power for ill, but shamanism itself is not thought of as demonic.

Eventually, the popular image of the wizard became that of a bearded, dishevelled old man, who should be invited to weddings and family rituals as an insurance policy to make sure of keeping his continued good favour. But the wizard has survived, continuing to exist within village life, along with his female counterpart of the wise woman healer or diviner. Urban wizards, modern-day magicians, are also thriving, whether or not they base their sorcery on traditional practice; as a Russian colleague, Vlad Shilinis, now domiciled in the USA, tells me:

> They are not only found in remote parts but in towns and cities, from fake to talented and from black to white. If you don't believe me, check the ad section in the Russian newspapers. Of course, they are not the real stuff but it proves the point — the market for magic in Russia is huge. Russians were always very fond or afraid of them, from common people to the highest political élite, even in Soviet times. For instance, Brehznev used one and everybody knew about it.

The local healers may not reveal themselves so readily though, he tells me, and will withdraw when strangers are present. However, his wife Natalia Danilin was brought up within the tradition. Her own mother studied these healing arts, based on magic, prayer and herbalism, and was referred to as a *znaharka*, a word which comes from the verb 'to know.' *Znaharki* are thus the women who know. Natasha's account of her mother's skills, and the healing spell she passed down to her daughter, are worth setting out in full:

> My mother was a *znaharka* in her own right. In spite of having university education and being a mathematician and a party member(!) she was very keen on learning from wise women and knew many of them. So I understood that they had a kind of underground network and learned from each other. That is, if one *znaharka* or

> simply *babushka* (grandmother or old woman) didn't know how to treat any particular illness, the patient was sent to another *babushka* who knew the treatment and so on. My mother knew how to get rid of warts, 'lichen' (a term for any of several eruptive skin diseases), boils, rheumatic fever, and how to treat deep wounds, diabetes and gangrene. As far as I remember every treatment commenced with 'Hail Mary ...' Her greatest achievement was the health of my father who came home after the war dying of wounds and diabetes. His condition was so bad, that the Soviet hospitals refused to take him as 'terminally ill'. My mother kept him alive with her herbs and spells for nineteen years! Our house was a virtual herbal factory with drying herbs all over the place, which she gathered in the woods, meadows and from her own garden. I still remember the wonderful fragrance of drying herbs in her house.
>
> When I was about to emigrate, she said: 'Daughter, I don't have anything to give you as a parting gift but this. Use it when you are in big trouble,' and handed me an old Slavonic magic spell. I used it few times and it works very well. I can't give you the text, but can tell you that it is beautiful and begins with invocation of powers of Mother of God. However the text itself is definitely not in the Bible or any prayer book. She died in her sleep with a smile on her face. I am sending you her photograph taken shortly before she died. It is hard not to notice a kind of aura of blessedness around her. At least, this is what I feel about her. (see Fig.14)

Natasha also wrote to me about her own healing from a traditional village *znaharka:*

> In the fifties, in the Volga region in Russia, I found out that my mother knew a *znaharka*. She said that this healer, who was 88 years old, had treated almost all our family members: my elder sister, brother and my other sister who had a thyroid problem. My sister didn't believe in

> the healer since she was an educated girl and a biologist, but the surgery was cancelled because the problem disappeared somehow. My brother's hernia vanished as well after her treatment.
>
> I got scabies in Leningrad and tried to get medical help but it was taking too long, so I went to Saratov to see my mother, who sent me to the *znaharka.* She was a small wiry old woman who didn't take the money I offered, so I handed it to her daughter. Then she slowly made a ball out of a rough thread, murmuring something under her breath. Next she rubbed this ball all over my skin saying 'Hail Mary, Mother of God ...' aloud, buried the ball in the soil and said that the problem would go away in a few days. She also told me to buy butter, mix it with sulphur powder and rub it into the skin. So I did. The scabies promptly disappeared in three days.

The *znaharka* complained that she couldn't die because she couldn't get the right apprentice. Her daughter didn't want to learn her Art. She invited Natasha to study with her, but Natasha didn't take up the offer. However, till this day, she regrets the missed opportunity.

The traditional village *koldun,* or sorcerer, took a more prominent part in local ceremonies, especially in wedding customs, where one of his chief tasks was to ward off any evil that might befall the bride and groom, who are vulnerable to ill wishers and the evil eye of the envious on their wedding day. He also assisted with the pre-nuptial rituals. On the eve of the wedding, he might conduct the bride through her bathhouse rites, as we have already seen in Chapter 3, or bless the carriages in the bridal procession, and cast straw beneath the feet of the bride to protect her innocence as she walked to meet her groom. He could even be responsible for accompanying the newly-married pair to the bedchamber, and would there circle around them, chanting a prayer of protection as they prepared for the consummation of their union (see Ryan 1999, p.74).

There is also some evidence that there was interaction between magical practitioners. It is recorded that sorcerers sometimes banded together, often to do battle with witches, considering that they themselves were forces for good, and that witches acted for evil ends. It is probably this shadowy tradition which is at the root of the comic *lubok* woodcut, mentioned above, where Baba Yaga, the prototype Russian witch, rides out on a hairy pig to do battle with a magician. Wizards and witches were also said to be closely allied with the animal kingdom. Witches were thought to change into magpies, and wizards into wolves, and in this form the magpies could fly around in flocks, and the wolves come together in packs. The ancient *bogatyr* hero, Volkh Vseslavyevich, his name identifying him as 'Wizard of the Slavs', had to learn how to turn himself into a wolf in order to acquire the three 'wisdoms' necessary in becoming a fully-fledged magician-hero. Wizards tended to look something like their wolf familiar, with their penetrating eyes, shaggy manes of hair, and unkempt beards. The unshaven locks represented their power, which might be lost if their hair was cut. As for tails, some wizards, it is said, are born with tails, and those that aren't may acquire them at their initiation ceremony.[6]

Wolves are considered to be magical shape-shifters themselves; Grey Wolf, who we met in the story of *Prince Ivan and the Firebird,* is able to change himself into the likeness of the beautiful princess Elena, in order to deceive the king who has been courting her, so that Prince Ivan may carry off the real princess for himself. The line between wolves and wizards therefore seems to be a fluid one, and you may never be sure, if you encounter a wolf, that it is not a wizard glaring at you with yellow eyes, or, in reverse, if there is a wolf's spirit hidden beneath the rough mane and fierce stare of the local wizard.

The Evil Eye and the magic doll

The Evil Eye is still considered a powerful force in Russia, as much in the suburbs of Moscow as in country areas. The daughter of some Russian friends of mine had just got married in an urban registry office, where she had looked stunning, with her long blonde hair and tall, slim figure elegantly dressed in white satin. In fact, she looked so beautiful that the registrar asked afterwards if they could display her wedding photo on the wall of the marriage office.

'But we said no,' her mother told me.

'Why?' I was surprised, as this was a daughter and a wedding to be proud of.

She looked uncomfortable. 'Perhaps it's hard for you to understand,' she said. 'But we have these beliefs — that if her picture is there, and someone is envious, they could cause some bad luck to happen to her.'

Much of the wizard's involvement at weddings was to prevent such an occurrence, and to counter the possible force of evil magic with stronger magic of his own. Belief in the Evil Eye is widespread not only in Russia but in the Middle and Far East, and talismans in the form of an eye (such as the popular blue and white glass 'magic eye' sold in Turkey) are thought to ward off the potential harm that surrounds us. In Russia itself, peasants used to hang up bear skulls in the farmyard to avert the evil eye; the bear, as we shall see shortly, is a formidable source of magic in its own right. The eye symbolizes the unwanted or envious attention of others, which is thought to be capable of penetrating our psyche, and doing us harm. If someone feels affected by the evil eye in Russia, a simple and popular way of dispelling this is to put on one's coat using the right arm first, if the left is usually the first to go into the sleeve, or vice versa. Reversals are a traditional way of either creating magic, or undoing its effects.

And perhaps the power of the eye to gaze inside us can be too great, even if no harm is intended. A doll's eyes, it is thought, can upset a little child and do damage, so dolls that are given to very small children in Russia traditionally have no features, and certainly no eyes marked. The magic doll carried by Vasilisa the Fair in her encounter with Baba Yaga may also have power in its gaze, in this case to avert the Evil Eye. The eyes of the doll act on behalf of Vasilisa herself, returning the witch's gaze, protecting Vasilisa from Baba Yaga's spell, and also creating an effective magic of their own. It is the doll that finally forces the witch to release Vasilisa; when she finds out that it is helping and protecting Vasilisa, she releases the girl from captivity, as the blessing the doll has received from Vasilisa's mother on her death bed is too strong for her to contend with.

The doll may itself be a form of wise woman's amulet, or shamanic talisman. It is common for a shaman to give someone a spirit pouch or bag after a session, as I discovered with Herel, the Siberian shaman. After the séance, he handed me a small cloth bag decorated with a few beads, and tied up with a plaited cord. 'Hang it above your bed,' he instructed me. 'And you can take it with you when you go somewhere on business. It will help to protect you, but you must feed it with drops of melted butter every few days.' I did as he suggested, and had a series of vivid dreams full of strange imagery soon afterwards, which lasted for weeks, and included one about giant white dragonflies. I later discovered in my reading that there is an order of shamans who are said to take this form of the white dragonfly in their trance state. The butter was more difficult, as a little went a long way, and the pouch soon became rather smelly as it went rancid. To my senses, the talisman did seem to have a life and energy of its own, (apart from the smell), which died away after a year or so, at which point I laid it carefully away in a drawer.

Divination

Divination is a foray into the 'otherworld', an excursion beyond the boundaries of everyday life. It has probably been practised in all societies, and at all periods of history, and although some may regard it as mere superstition, a more thoughtful approach, and one more in tune with contemporary studies of consciousness, is to see it as a way of venturing to make a connection to other realms of time and space than those which we normally inhabit.[7] As I wrote in my earlier study of the practice of divination:

> To divine is to journey into the unknown. Divination involves travelling beyond the limits of ordinary, rational knowledge into a realm where we may discover knowledge not usually accessible to us. We hope there to catch a glimpse of what is, what has been and what will be. We dare to venture into it because ...we can sense that

> our normal perceptions of time and events are limited, describing only the outlines of a three-dimensional reality ... Divination, in its truest sense, is to know the divine. (Gilchrist 1987, p.7)

In Russian traditions, divination practices can vary from the intensity of shamanic trance, during which the shaman leaves his or her ordinary body to penetrate the spirit world and ask for indications of coming events, to a bunch of giggling girls having an enjoyable time telling fortunes, and perhaps scaring themselves a little into the bargain. Although the full shamanic tradition has been lost in the main territory of Russia, the professional fortune-teller, usually known as the *vorozheia,* has been a part of society down through the centuries (see Fig. 6). And at the level of the common people, divination practices were and still are available; there are a multitude of examples of folk divination, many recorded by folklorists past and present, some of which are still current today.

'When we were young, we used to make garlands out of flowers or leaves,' a sophisticated Russian lady, now a concert pianist, told me. 'Then we would drop them into the river and see which way they floated. That was meant to tell us what would happen in our love life.'

The tradition is echoed in a folk song which accompanies the practice of throwing wreaths or garlands into the water:

I, a young girl, am going to the quiet meadow,
to a little birch.
I, a young girl, will pluck a blue cornflower,
a little blue flower.
I, a young girl, will weave a wreath,
I, a young girl, will go to the river,
I will throw the wreath down the river.
I will think about my sweetheart:
My wreath is drowning, drowning,
My heart is aching, aching.
My wreath will drown,
My sweetheart will abandon me.

On my first visit to Russia in 1992, (the first of over fifty visits), I came across two bashful teenage girls in a local park, who had crowned themselves with wreaths beautifully made from autumn leaves. Were they, perhaps, on their way to the nearest lake or stream to tell their fortune from the waters?

In Russia, the inheritors of the divination traditions are often girls, who are, after all, eternally curious about the future of love in their lives. In the West, most of the old divination practices seem to have been reduced to a few children's games: I remember being initiated into the rite of counting prune stones at a very young age after eating my school dinner: 'Who will I marry? Tinker, tailor, soldier, sailor, rich man, poor man, beggar man, thief. What will I marry in? Silk, satin, cotton, rags ...' and so on. The Russian tradition, on the other hand, is rich and varied, and it was an expected part of family and village life that groups of girls would sit in the attic playing at fortune-telling, or huddle around the stove on a winter's evening trying to work out who would be the first to marry. Though mostly a girls' game, the boys might join in too, as we have seen in the case of the bathhouse (see Chapter 3, p.62). And if relegated to girls, and if a lot of laughter and fun was had, this does not mean that Russian traditional divination became superficial and frivolous. Any attempt at divination carries with it a certain *frisson,* a certain sensation that now you may know, now you will find that slender wisp of truth that has been eluding you, now the curtain will be pulled back just a little way so that you can see into the future. And nor was it an exclusive pastime for girls: the former Soviet politician, Andrei Gromyko (1909–89) mentions in his memoirs that he was keen to find out his marriage prospects, and, following the local tradition, set off for the bathhouse at night carrying a torch and a mirror. Once there, he extinguished the torch and placed the mirror opposite the open door, as custom decreed. Then he had to wait in the dark in the deserted bathhouse until midnight, at which time the face of his future spouse would allegedly appear in the mirror. But young Andrei was so terrified that he couldn't hold out for the appointed hour, and fled for home, none the wiser (quoted in Ryan 1999, p.100).

A more picturesque form of divination is to place little candles in walnut shells, light them, and set them floating in a bowl of water. Girls sit around the bowl, watching their own designated shell intently to see what will happen. The first flame to go out signifies the first girl to marry, though, as with the garlands in the river, for the shell to sink is a bad sign, and usually means that the girl will remain unmarried. Another custom is to drop molten wax, or lead, or egg white into water, and to study the shapes created, which are said to reveal the future. The shapes can be interpreted according to local lore: a cross may mean a hard life; a crown, marriage; and a coffin, death, for instance. Or they may be used for a kind of free form divination, to see what images come to mind from shapes in the water, and to interpret them as prognostications of future events. This can also be done by gazing into smoke, flames, or clouds. Such free-form methods of scrying are not exclusive to the Russian tradition, and are probably as old as humankind.[8]

Some Russian practices have died out in the modern age for practical reasons; one of these was to listen for bells at a crossroads (considered to be a liminal, magical place since antiquity in human culture), and interpret the future from their sound. Today, there are few carts and troikas arriving whose horses are bedecked with bells, and anyone placing an ear to the ground at a modern Russian crossroads is likely to be run over in a trice by a speeding car or lorry thundering by. Another common form of divination involving listening, which is unlikely to become obsolete, is to eavesdrop on the conversations of passers-by. The words overheard are given oracular status — mention of a shirt means death, of a forest, good fortune, and of a marsh, bad luck.

In other ritualized practices, chickens might be offered a scattering of corn, and the future judged by the place they choose to peck at. As well as using ritual or invocations, divination is often hallowed by choosing a special day in the year to carry it out, such as St John's Eve (Midsummer), for instance, when girls can place twelve designated magical herbs under their pillows, and hope to see their future husband in a dream. Although trying to divine the identity of your future spouse is probably the commonest form of divination, there are other key purposes: to know who will die first in the family or village, to know what kind of weather to expect, to detect a thief, or to discover the sex of an unborn child, for example.

Rituals of folk divination are thus legion in the Russian tradition, and although most today are practised by girls and young women, with a fair number of young men joining in too, this is not exclusively their province. There are also old women living in remote villages who still conduct divination practices for the benefit of their communities (at New Year, for instance, to give prognostications for the coming twelve months), and who may be regularly visited by teams of ethnographers, eager to record the ways of old Russia for posterity. According to one source, these local soothsayers are visited secretly by all different kinds of people in the village, not only young girls but married women, and men both young and old (Rozhnova 1992, p.22). My own impression is that while specific rites and divination customs may die out over the years, there is still a strong tradition of divination alive in Russia, which shows itself not only in old folk methods, but also in imported forms (in Russian terms), such as astrology and Tarot readings. It would be artificial to make a division between the two, because the heart of the matter, that keeps any form of divination or clairvoyance alive, is the Russian love of the mysterious, the reverence for the spirit that goes beyond the commonplace, and the eagerness to penetrate the realms of the otherworld.

Mishka the Bear

Bears are creatures popularly believed in Russia to inhabit that otherworld, and they are treated with awe and respect, not only for their formidable strength, but also for their supernatural powers. The word for bear in Russian is *medved,* or 'honey knower', which of course goes with the bear's fondness for searching out sweet things, especially honey. One inhabitant of a Russian village in the north told me that bears steal raspberries from their gardens in summer, and what with that and wolves creeping up close to their homes in winter, they have a real need of their dogs to warn them of intruders from the wilds. But although officially called *medved,* as a sacred animal, the bear's real name must not be spoken aloud, so traditionally it has always been known as Mishka. Mishka is a playful diminutive, a masculine name, and from this mixture of playfulness and fear, respect and defensiveness, the Russian relationship with the bear is formed.

The cult of the bear in Russia goes back to pre-history, as indeed it does in other countries where people and bears may once have shared different areas of the same cave as living quarters; this co-existence may have brought an uneasy truce, and perhaps in some cases the taming of bear cubs. Although in modern times we may recoil from seeing performing bears in circuses and tame bears at tourist sites, it is helpful to keep in mind that there is in fact a genuine relationship between the human handler and the bear, and in the best cases there can be a real empathy between them. I have by contrast seen a terribly cruel example of a bear kept in a tiny cage by the side of a scruffy roadside restaurant, sitting in blazing sunshine with no shade, while visitors peered and prodded at it. But I have also seen performances in the top Russian circuses which seem to depend on co-operation between the handler and the bear, and where the bears are treated kindly and allowed to retain their dignity. I make no appeal to continue public performances with bears, but only wish to suggest that any real and long-term relationship between human beings and animals should at least be understood in its historical and mythological context. The occasional bear tamer you may see walking the streets today is a direct descendant of the old wandering entertainers of Russia, who travelled the unpaved roads with their bears, and were warmly greeted by villagers everywhere, who welcomed bears as lucky bringers of wealth and fertility. The lives of humans and bears were considered to be so intertwined, that Eastern Slavs believed bears to be their ancestors.

The bear hunt once played a significant part in Russian life. Even though the aim of the hunt was to kill, all hunters had to show respect for the animals they tracked down, for instance by giving a feast for the slain bear at which it was ceremonially displayed; guests had to pay tribute to it by bowing low, and kissing its muzzle in homage. Hunters were also wary of the spirit of the bear, which they believed might take its revenge, so various rituals or decoy activities were employed to prevent it from seeking out its killers. A hunter confronted with the spirit of the angry departed bear would say: 'It wasn't me that killed you! It was the men from the other tribe!' Another rather more eerie custom was to take the bear's skin into the house by passing it through a window; this prevented its spirit from following the skin indoors, as it could only enter through a doorway. The revenge of the bear could be terrible. A Siberian legend tells of a hunter who desecrated the body of a bear by using its front paws as brooms, and its back paws as shovels around the home. The angry bear spirit turned up with a whole posse of fighting bears, determined to wreak their vengeance, and despite pleas from the hunter for forgiveness, the bear smashed down his house and killed him.

In this particular story, the bear originally comes from the heavenly regions, and descends to earth through a hole in the sky. But it is primarily an underworld or otherworld creature, regarded as such because it hibernates under the ground in winter and reemerges in the spring. Its reappearance was once greeted with celebratory dances, in which the movements imitated those of the bear. This association with the renewal of the seasons also gives it a vital link with fertility, and so it is the creature most closely connected with rampant sexual activity in folklore; in some parts of Russia, newlyweds are still referred to as 'bears'.[9] By the same token, the bear is associated with rebirth, representing the life that springs up anew from the ground after dwelling in the dark unseen regions of the dead.

I was aware of this highly charged mythology surrounding the bear when I participated in a private séance with the shaman in southern Siberia, and so I sat down on the bear's skin spread out for me on the floor with some trepidation. I did not feel that it was disrespectful to use a bear's hide in this context, as I knew that the shamans honoured the spirits of animals and birds, but I wondered about the lingering spirit of the bear, and also had to overcome my Western distaste of slaughtered creatures, which meant trying to accept sitting on the soft warm fur of the bear as part of genuine shamanic experience. Once I had adjusted to this, it was a strangely comforting feeling, in fact. I relaxed into the session, bathed in the sound of chanting and drumming, only to be jolted some minutes later by a sudden thump between my shoulder blades. Afterwards, I discovered that this had been done with a bear's paw. It was heavy and abrupt, but not unpleasant, and the amount of force that was used felt just right. Herel later explained that he measures the blows with the bear's paw according to the impact that each person needs; later that day, as he conducted a well-wishing ceremony for visitors at the local yurt camp, he processed around the circle of people touching some lightly with the bear's paw, and giving others a mighty whack between the shoulders.

In a shamanic session, the person receiving treatment (usually to clear away bad energy, and to restore vitality and health) may thus literally sit on the back of the bear, and perhaps this is related to a number of stories told in Russia, in which a bear carries a young girl off on his back. The bear's usual aim is to take her back to his kingdom, and make her his bride. Sometimes he is under a spell of enchantment, and all ends well when he is returned to his original shape as a handsome young man. Sometimes the bear perishes, dying of love for the maiden he has kidnapped. In this mythological tradition, the bear is not seen as a subtle or perceptive creature; his emotions are certainly powerful when roused, and he can be loving and angry in great measure, but he may also be clumsy in executing his intentions. Bears in lighter-hearted animal folktales are often portrayed as stupid for this reason, and can be outwitted by a cunning human, or another clever animal such as a fox. And humans who behave badly, acting out of rapacious greed, for instance, may be turned into bears as a punishment.

Mishka the bear is thus a powerful figure in Russian mythology, who comes lumbering out of the underworld and roams through the forest, hungry for the sweetness of honey, and for the yet untested sweetness of innocent maidens. He may be either friend or foe, and in pitting yourself against him in the hunt you are taking on a fearsome challenge. But the bear spirit, placated and tamed, brings with it the blessings of fertility, and of the renewal of the seasons and the good fortune of the community. The bear descends into the shadows to bring out from them the gift of life.

Koshchei the Deathless, and the Egg of Life

> In the middle of the great ocean there is an island; on the island stands a mighty oak tree; at the foot of that tree, a chest is buried; in the chest is a hare; in the hare is a duck; in the duck is an egg, and in the egg lies my death. (Warner 1985, p.98)

So speaks the terrible Koshchei the Deathless, inadvertently betraying the secret of his future death to the beautiful Princess Vasilisa, who he is holding in captivity. She manages to relay it to her lover, Prince Ivan, and his heroic helper, Bulat the Brave, and, with this knowledge, the three of them are able to outwit the tyrant, engineering her escape from his clutches. They finally kill the fiend by smashing him over the head with the mythical egg that contains his death.

Koshchei the Deathless is a familiar figure in Russian folktales. He is a fearful adversary, who represents death itself; he is a creature of old bones and shrivelled skin, who appears to be hanging on to life by a thread, and he is ready to destroy anyone else who crosses his path. But the bringer of death is himself indestructible, unless you can find out the secret of where his death is to be found. This does not lie in his body, but elsewhere; sometimes it is in the tip of a needle, but most often it is hidden in an egg that is concealed within other symbolic forms of life — in this case a duck, a hare and the roots of an oak tree.[10] If the hero of the story can find that egg, confront Koshchei, and break it over his head, he will be vanquished. Life can thus conquer death, we might say; within this egg that represents the very germ of life, the death of death itself lies.

Although Koshchei is the image of living death, he has his own zest for life, and a strong desire for beautiful young women, who he is fond of abducting when he can. In the story of Maria Morevna, the warrior princess, her husband Prince Ivan encounters the fearful Koshchei while his wife is away at war. Much as Maria loves him, she cannot resist setting off for battle every now and then, and she tells Ivan that while she is away, he can go into every room in her palace except for one. Ivan ignores the warning, and cannot resist unlocking the door of that forbidden chamber.

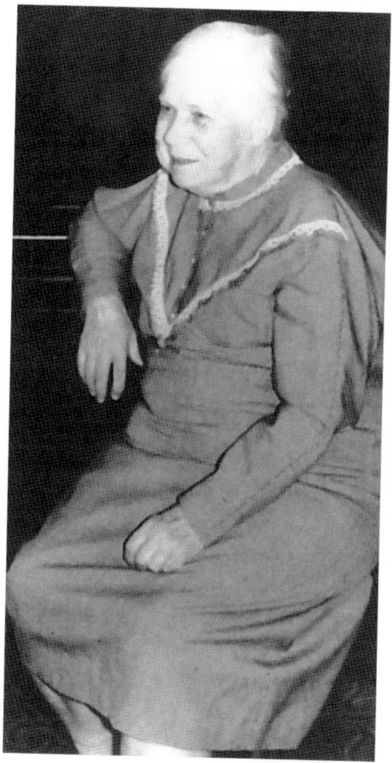

Fig. 14 — Natasha's mother, a *znaharka,* or wise woman. See. p. 108.

Fig. 15 — An old man shows his grandson the secrets of the forest. See p. 127.

Fig. 16 — Older folk enjoy themselves at the Maslnitsa festival, singing to the *garmon*, a type of small accordion. See p. 152.

Fig. 17 — A scene of Maslnitsa festivities. *(Lacquer miniature from Mstiora.)* See p. 153.

Fig 18. — Lenin, the Communist leader, who himself became the stuff of legend. *(Lacquer miniature from Fedoskino.)* See p. 22.

Fig. 19 — The ceremony of Bread and Salt, offered as a welcome. See p. 50.

Fig. 20 — The sacred Red Corner of the home with family icon, ceremonial towel and birch leaves to celebrate Trinity Sunday. See p. 45.

Fig. 21 — Khokhloma ware, with its combination of red, gold and black ornament. See p. 67.

Fig. 22 — Divination in the Mirror, looking for signs of a future husband. *(Lacquer miniature from Fedoskino.)* See p. 56.

Fig. 23 — The *khorovod*, or women's circle dance; a spontaneous dance at a birthday party. See p. 155.

Fig. 24 — Matrioshka nesting dolls, with hen motif as a symbol of happiness. See p. 33.

Fig. 25 — Learning forest-lore with Svetlana, a nurse who gave up her profession to study the ancient Russian ways of healing. See p. 60.

Fig 26 — The results of a mushroom gathering expedition. See p. 127.

Fig. 27 — The mighty figure of Father Frost, who presides over the New Year festivities. *(Lacquer miniature from Kholui.)* See p. 157.

Fig. 28 — The story of Emelya and the Magic Pike. *(Lacquer miniature from Kholui.)* See p. 141

Fig. 29 — St John's Eve: searching for the Flowers of Fire at the Midsummer Festival. *(Lacquer miniature from Kholui.)* See p. 82.

Fig. 30 — Image of the Mother Goddess embroidered on a linen towel, with Tree of Life, and horses and peacock as sky spirits. See p. 25.

Inside, he discovers Koshchei the Deathless, who is imprisoned there, tied up to the wall with twelve strong chains. Koshchei, groaning in torment, pleads with Ivan for water, claiming that he has been held captive for ten years with nothing to eat or drink. Ivan does not recognize who the old man is, and in his naivety brings him three pails of water, which Koshchei gulps down one after the other, growing stronger with each mouthful until at last he bursts out of his chains and escapes through the window in the form of a whirlwind, something often associated with demons and devils (see Chapter 4, p.86). He catches up with Maria Morevna and carries her off, leaving Ivan in hot pursuit. After various challenges, such as the encounter with Baba Yaga described earlier, Ivan finally manages to rescue his wife and vanquish Koshchei. In this case, it is not an egg that contains his death, but a kick from the hoof of the magical horse that Prince Ivan is riding; in both instances, though, it is a blow to the head that finishes off the evil monster.

The egg in Russia has long been associated with life, as indeed it is in many traditions. Eggs are often coloured for Easter, blessed in church, and used for Easter games, just as they are in the West. But as the festival of Easter is much more prominent in the Orthodox calendar and more widely celebrated than Christmas, this gives the egg an even greater significance in Russian culture. It also has a correspondingly prominent place in folk art, so that as a visitor to Russia you can buy wooden eggs cheerfully painted with fairy tale scenes or country landscapes. Icons are sometimes painted on eggs too, and you can find exquisite miniature replicas of Fabergé eggs on offer, not to mention the Fabergé egg originals that may be seen in museums.

Perhaps the unique feature of the egg in the Russian tradition is that it is used to symbolize not just new life, but the connection between life and death. At the ancient, probably pre-Christian, festival of the dead, known as *Radunitsa,* people gather in graveyards and cemeteries where they feast among the graves of their ancestors, leaving them gifts of eggs. This was once a very popular custom, accompanied by ritual lamenting which mourns the passing of loved ones, but the eggs offered seem to promise the start of new life for the departed. Both this custom, and the stories told about Koshchei are, to my mind, a curious mirroring of life and death, in which they reflect each other backwards and forwards, creating more than a simple polarization of two opposing forces, and revealing the eternal flowing of one to the other, in which they are forever connected. In one, you see the seeds of the other, and although either life or death may predominate at any one time, the balance never finally tips, and neither gains ultimate supremacy.

6

The Enchanted Landscape

The Russian landscape

The scenery of central Russia is a mixture of forest and open grasslands, set in gently undulating countryside, and interspersed with short stretches of heath and marsh. Wide rivers flow slowly and majestically through the landscape, joined by smaller streams and rivers which amble rather than race towards their destination. In some areas, lakes abound, and everywhere smaller pools, fringed by reeds and yellow flags, appear in meadows and woods. There is plenty of bird life; you may see a flock of cranes descend into a meadow full of wild blue lupins, a woodpecker eyeing you curiously at the edge of the forest, or a moth-like nightjar sitting on a garden fence. In winter, the *snegir* or Russian bullfinch is a welcome sight, red-breasted, feasting on the last of the rowanberries. For humans, the landscape is also a generous provider, as the forests and thickets are full of nuts and berries — bilberries, cranberries, raspberries, hazel nuts and wild strawberries growing in the depths of the forest, or along its margins.

This is a beautiful landscape in winter, too, when frost coats the delicate branches of the trees, and snowy vistas glint like diamonds during the short hours of daylight, and harbour the burning colours of the setting sun in pools of molten gold. But perhaps it is on an early summer's morning that you may see it at its best, dawn fresh and filmy green, wisps of mist floating over the meadows that are studded with wild flowers, and the first rays of the sun catching the dew in the grass and dancing on the leaves of tall lime trees, broad oak and graceful birch. It is a landscape beloved by the Russian people, a kind of nature that is both intimate and open, with detail as delicate as lace close to, and opening up to a larger scale beyond, to a vast land of distant regions over the horizon. This combination of woodland, grassland and water forms the basic trilogy of the Russian landscape, found in its quintessential form in the central areas of the country. Of the three elements, it is forest and water that are the chief repository of traditional lore, and it is these which will be explored here in greatest depth.

Each area in Russia is also considered to have its own unique spirit of place, and this is particularly notable in terms of local arts or crafts, which are said to be born out of the landscape, and to receive continual inspiration from it. As one lacquer miniature artist put it:

> The spirit of place is really very important. I felt it acutely when I left Palekh for two months. And I couldn't work, I couldn't create anything. It's important because as well as the people who work alongside you, there is a special rhythm to life. (Andrei Petrov, Palekh, 1995)

In Russia, one's identity becomes infused with this spirit of place, and to leave it means leaving part of one's soul behind. As we have already seen, Russian people are sensitive to energies, and take account of what could be called the spiritual geography of a locality. Perhaps this capacity is inherited directly from the ancient Slavs, and linked to a time when nature was experienced with complete immediacy, and as an animate force. Although the early animistic religion of Russia is largely lost to us now, a sense of it remains, and the landscape is still perceived as embodying contours of spirit, and as hosting a variety of nature spirits and minor deities.

Nature spirits

After the animistic or shamanic religion was supplanted in Russia, and after the subsequent pantheon of Slavic gods was displaced by the coming of Christianity, certain forms of these old religions remained, becoming part of common belief, and forming what we might call 'the Russian native tradition'. The chief survivors in the landscape itself are the Russian nature spirits, as they are generally called. Some authorities may see these as representing deposed gods and goddesses, whereas others view them more as elemental forces of nature personified, but their place in traditional Russian belief was firmly held and undisputed until well on in the twentieth century. Even now, the belief persists, and sophisticated young people are as likely to believe in nature spirits as their rural-dwelling grandmothers (see Chapter 3). We have already met the *bannik,* the spirit of the bathhouse, and the *domavoi,* the spirit of the home, who belong to the legion of nature spirits; later in this chapter we shall meet spirits who inhabit the forests and the rivers.

Nature spirits are attached to a particular type of location, and vivid descriptions are given of their appearance. However, these descriptions can vary widely, suggesting that in most cases the nature spirits are shape-shifters, who can take on a variety of guises. They are certainly tricksy creatures, and often capricious and wilful; it is wise to be on one's guard, while at the same time showing them due respect, as the real life story of the young man and *bannik* reveals (see p.63). These nature spirits are legion: there are specific types of spirits which inhabit the field, forest, river, home, bathhouse, courtyard, and barnyard, to mention but a few. They are both generic and specific, so that, for instance, *polevoi,* the spirit of the field, has the general characteristics of being an ugly little creature, with earth coloured skin and green grass growing on his head, but each field or group of fields harbours its own, individual *polevoi,* and sometimes his wife and children too.

Now that a broad view of the Russian landscape and its inhabitants has been given, we can move on to explore certain aspects of it in depth, those which are most strongly infused with a sense of myth and mystery, and which play the strongest part in Russian traditions.

The life of the forest

> When I go to the forest, I often reach very isolated places that other people rarely visit. And something there reminds me of the time before Christianity came

> to Russia, and I think that maybe this is a place where, long ago, in pagan times, my ancient ancestors sat around the fire. Such feelings come to me particularly at sunset. (Andrei Petrov, Palekh 1995)

The forest is a world in its own right, beloved by Russian people, frequented for solace, reflection, celebration, and more practically, as a source of food. It is a link to their past, as artist Andrei Petrov describes above, for in the early days the Slavs lived in stockade camps or villages in the forest, from where they hunted through its stretches, fended off wild beasts and used its wood as the basic material for constructing their lives. Russian people today still instinctively head for the forest: 'It's where you go to shake off the cares of everyday life,' I was told.

And on one frosty New Year's Day, I accompanied my host family on a long walk from the village into the depths of the forest, for there was no question about where we would celebrate this first day of the coming year. After much debate about the right spot to choose, a small clearing near the edge of the forest was selected. An axe was produced, a dead tree chopped down, cut into logs, and used to make a bonfire, in the same way that this has been done for hundreds of years. (Carrying an axe on an expedition in Russia, even for a modest picnic, is standard practice, and a few years ago 'green police' were installed in one of Moscow's parks to try and prevent the practice of city residents of cutting down its trees for a bonfire every time they came there for a picnic.)

With the flames blazing, we toasted the New Year and each other in vodka — essential to warm us up, of course, in the snowy weather — then linked arms, and danced around the bonfire. We consumed a feast of boiled eggs, salami sandwiches, potato salad, cake and fruit, and sang folksongs until our toes turned numb and the sky began to grow red at the approach of the early midwinter sunset. Bonfire doused, bottles stacked around the base of the tree, in the fond belief that Mother Earth will somehow deal with the debris, we marched home, briskly now, with the approach of darkness and a sharp frost hastening our footsteps. A fierce red light still glowered on the horizon, but as we approached the village, the little windows in the wooden houses began to turn gold, shining with lamplight to welcome us back. It was a New Year celebration that will stay in my mind forever, bringing us into magical union with the forest and the timeless spirit of Russian life.

People have their own traditions connected with the forest (see Fig. 15). In one family, the father always goes out into the forest in late December with his youngest daughter, to choose a fir tree to bring home and decorate for their New Year festivities. Another family told me how they select their future New Year's tree when it is still a sapling; they choose one that is off the beaten track, growing deep in the forest where no one else is likely to spot it, and they keep an eye on it until it is just the right height to cut down and bring home.

Forest is just 'forest', or *les,* in Russia. It is not named, as far as I am aware, in the same way that we give names to woodland in England, such as Sherwood Forest or Wistman's Wood. Once forest *was* the land, and this is still the instinctive understanding in northern and central Russia, that it is the origin of life, and the place to which one returns, both for sustenance and to attune to the timeless soul of the land. People return to the forest not only in life but in death too, for most Russian burials are made in cemeteries in the forest. Even on an almost tree-less island in a northern lake, I saw that two or three rowan trees standing on a rocky outcrop had been chosen as guardians of the small burial ground there. And, as mentioned earlier, wooden villages are both born out of the forest and decay back into it again.

The forest is always present; in central Russia, if you are not already in it, you can nearly always see forest on the horizon, and in northern Russia, you may well be living in it: 'Northern Russia is to this day largely enveloped in a huge coniferous forest: the greatest forest in the world, stretching from Scandinavia to the Pacific' (Milner-Gulland 1997, p.6). Central Russian forest is usually mixed, with lime, birch, oak, rowan and hazel all playing a part, as well as coniferous trees such as pine and fir. It is a rich source of berries and mushrooms, and every true-blooded Russian will head out into the forest on a warm, damp day in summer or early autumn to search for some of the two hundred and fifty or so edible fungi that grow there (see Fig. 26). Most families have their own mushrooming traditions, recognizing and picking perhaps twenty types that they can identify with confidence. One of the great favourites is the boletus known as *beli,* a word meaning 'white', used even though the fungus is shiny brown; this is perhaps because to call something 'white' is a high accolade, and these mushrooms are prized for their superior flavour and texture. Mushroom treks involve wearing sensible clothing for pushing through forest scrub, and carrying woven birch baskets which keep the mushrooms fresh and intact. A sharp knife is also essential, for skilful picking requires that you sever the mushroom near its base just above the ground, leaving the portion underground unharmed to grow another year.

It did not take much to encourage a Russian friend, Sergey Mukhin, to write to me about his mushroom hunting experiences, in enthusiastic if inaccurate English:

> By the way, there is only one really poisonous mushroom. We call it pale *poganka* (biological name is Amanita phalloides). People can really die eating it. All the others are not so dangerous. For example, *moukhomor* this red one with white stains [known as fly agaric in English], people use in medicine and Vikings used it like drugs before battles. But, of course, it is necessary to be careful. For Russians it is easier, I was taken by my parents to the forest being three years old and, having a good memory and eyes, I'm sure that I'll never make a mistake. Also we had in the 1960s a lot of books with very nice pictures so I had nice practice and nice theoretical lessons. Now from time to time our newspapers write about some death because of mushrooms but we do have a lot of immigrants from former Soviet Asia Republics, they do not have good job and, living in the countryside, sometimes they try to feed themselves with help of mushrooms, but without any knowledge. Also it is necessary to know how to cook them in the right way. Some of them you can use without additional treatment, like *beli* but some of them it is necessary to boil or to put into the water for half of the week (usually they are for

> salting only). Sorry, that I write a lot about it. For me mushroom hunting is one of the best methods to have contact with nature and a nice rest.[1] (Email from Sergey Mukhin, September 11, 2003)

As a mushroom hunter in Russia on your way into the forest, you may meet other individuals or families emerging with their baskets full (or not) of mushrooms.

'*Dobri dyen!* Good day! How is it in the forest this morning?'

The emerging pickers shrug their shoulders, returning the greeting. '*Dobri dyen!* Oh well, not too bad. You know how it is.' They hurry on, reluctant to disclose where they might have been, their own favourite haunts where they have been searching for mushrooms for years. People have their own jealously guarded spots not only for mushrooms, but for picking bilberries, raspberries and wild strawberries too. If pressed, they will give only vague clues as to where they go, for these are family secrets passed down only to the children.

Once deep in the forest, it is easy to get lost. I was instructed how to search the forest for mushrooms by forming a long line with my companions, spread out so that we could not see each other, but remaining within shouting distance. Otherwise, you may lose track of your fellow pickers. One of the pictures sometimes painted on lacquer boxes shows a girl standing in the forest with a basket of mushrooms, trying to locate her friends; her hands cup her mouth as she calls out to them anxiously. On our expedition, I cut and picked mushrooms with delight, but when we rendezvoused to compare our finds, half of mine were tipped out unceremoniously onto the ground.

'*Poganka!* Toadstool!' pronounced Viktor, the leader of the expedition. Only a few approved specimens remained at the bottom of my basket, which was already a smaller version of the ones that the rest of the family carried. The sun was growing warm now, so we lay down in a grassy clearing on the forest outskirts to bask in its rays, and munch on a hearty breakfast brought in separate knapsacks.

'I remember once when I was walking through this forest,' Viktor said, 'and I came across a group of kids from the Children's

Home.' The old monastery in the village of Kholui had been turned into a home for orphaned and special needs children. 'They were sitting round in a circle, crying, because they had lost their way. It was lucky that I came across them — I was able to take them out of the forest and lead them back home again.'

The forest may also provide encounters with wild beasts, which can be startling, if not always downright dangerous. In central Russia, the risk of meeting bears or wolves these days is small, but it is not so uncommon to come across elks, huge and alarming in appearance, even if somewhat dozy in character. They venture inside the city boundaries of Moscow, and seem to enjoy the possibility of warmth generated by human life, even if they are not so keen on our company. Sergey, the mushroom hunter who lives in Moscow but frequently drives out into the country areas, wrote to me on the subject of the elk, after mentioning that he had met one on the road a few weeks earlier:

> As for elk, it is not very rare meeting on Russian roads, especially in provinces. But it can be a little dangerous in night time, when drivers see elks at last moment and in the case of mother-elk with baby. Fortunately, in February day was long enough to drive in the light time and it was man-elk. And I saw him from long distance. I did not understood at first what it was, but I saw something strange near the road. And it was nice to meet him in winter time. First, because it was possible to see him running away much longer, there are no leaves of the trees and bushes, second, it is very interesting to see how it runs in deep snow. After this it is easy to understand why elks have such long legs.
>
> Ivan Beketov (a colleague) said (to) me, that one frosty day he drove to Yuzha to his parents and also met elk. But his elk was not so frightened by car, more(over), elk came close to it and lay down on engine lid. Than after a minute stood up and walked away. Ivan thinks that elk decided to warm a little. (Email from Sergey Mukhin, March 5, 2004.)

The wood and the trees

The forest has provided the basic substance for life since time immemorial in Russia. Huts and houses are traditionally made of wood, while logs provide the fuel for the fires that are needed in winter. Drinking vessels, tubs, bowls and platters have all frequently been made of wood in times past, and transport was once dependent upon it, to make carts, sledges and boats. Not only trunks and planks are used, but birchbark (*beresta*) too is a superb material. It was used as an early form of paper in Russia, and its flexibility makes it ideal for weaving into shoes (*lapti*), baskets and storage canisters (see Fig. 13). It also makes good kindling for the stove.

Trees have specific associations; the oak, *dub,* as we have seen, represents the World Tree, and has its own spirit, Dubynia, a fierce and strong fellow who carries a wooden oak club over his shoulder. A fir tree may be a guardian spirit, planted in the farmyard not only for protection, but as a home for the *dvorovoi,* the nature spirit of the courtyard. Each type of wood has its own properties too in practical terms: lime and aspen are used for decorative carving, poplar for icon boards, pine for house building and furniture, for instance. But the birch is the best loved of all Russian trees. It is the national tree of Russia, known as *berioza,* or *beriozka* (little birch), and its gracefully hanging branches and lustrous grey and silver bark are seen as feminine attributions. It has longstanding associations with magic; garlands of birch twigs can be used for divination, and it is the focus of the girls' ritual on Trinity Sunday, as we shall see in the next chapter, a time when the birch is also brought into church in the form of young saplings or branches as part of the Whitsun celebrations.

The birch has many practical uses, and can also provide sap for a refreshing drink, as well as tar from its trunk. The old Russian word for April, *Berezozol,* actually means 'angry with birch trees', presumably relating to the fact that people cut deep into the wood of the trees to tap off the sap at this time of year, or felled them for their tar. Birch is thought of in general as a purifying force. The containers made of birch bark do indeed seem to have some antiseptic properties, and will conserve food such as sugar and flour for a long time; I store my biscuits in birch tubs and they remain fresh and crisp for many weeks. Farmers used to place twigs of birch in the corners of the homestead so that the cleansing spirit of the birch could heal and revive its energy, and the bathhouse today nearly always contains switches of leaves for use in washing, cleansing and gently whipping the body. In modern times, too, the sale of birch headbands has become popular, which are said to drive away headaches. As one traditional riddle about the birch has it: 'As I walked in the forest, I found a tree. This tree has three special powers: it lights, cures and cleans.'

Another tree honoured in the Russian tradition is the willow. Pussy willow has a special role in the Orthodox Calendar, and is used on Palm Sunday (palms being in short supply in such a northerly land) when the faithful carry a sprig with them to church. There it is blessed, and afterwards placed by the family icon at home. During the few days leading up to this festival in Moscow and St Petersburg, you may see country people standing doggedly outside metro stations and shopping centres, selling wands of pussy willow from the huge bunches that they have cut to bring into the city. Willow in general is considered to be beneficial to human welfare; three willow branches are said to clear a house of illness and misfortune, and a twig bound to your head with a cloth is reputed to be another sovereign remedy for a headache.

In the old days, it was said that the trees spoke and that people could talk to them. One tale relates how a woodcutter went into the forest to chop down trees, but every single tree he approached pleaded with him to spare its life. Each gave an excellent reason for its survival. The oak tree had acorns growing on it not yet ripe; without them, how could new oak trees grow? The alder needed to feed tiny wood bugs with its milk, and the aspen pointed out that the rustling of its leaves in the wind frightened away highwaymen at night: 'What is to become of good honest folk if I am chopped down?' The spruce wanted to grow to its full height, so that it could supply people with the wood for floor boards, and in the meantime gladden their hearts with its bright green branches. And the pine protested its superlative qualities: 'Of all the trees in the forest I do the greatest good. I bring good fortune to all and relief to sufferers from a hundred ailments.' (Having brought back bottles of locally produced pine oil from Siberia, I am ready to agree with that.) Finally, the spirit of the forest appears to the woodcutter, thanks him for his kindness in sparing the trees, and gives him a golden rod which will supply all his needs without having to chop any trees down at all.[2]

Such a story carries the sense of the forest as a living entity, as well as touching on the characteristics and spirit of each tree. The ideas it contains are not so far from those of contemporary ecology; they promote respect for living things and an understanding of the interrelationship between them. Perhaps it is not too far-fetched to say that nature lore in the Russian tradition creates a kind of traditional ecology, a way of teaching children, and indeed adults, that all interaction with nature must be on the basis of both give and take, and that we must protect the more vulnerable species, so as to preserve the whole web of life around us.

Leshii, the Forest Master

And what of the little man who greeted the woodcutter with a golden rod? This is *leshii,* nature spirit and forest master, who looks after all the birds, beasts, trees and plants in his domain. He is not just a creature of myth, but has regularly been seen by country folk; some of these reports of encounters with nature spirits have been recorded by ethnographers but, of course, many more are never written down, just passed on by word of mouth. One account that was recorded comes from an old woman in the Kaluga Province, who witnessed the appearance of *leshii* at the time of a great forest fire. 'He himself', as she referred to *leshii,* not daring to pronounce the name of a spirit, was 'as tall as a belltower.' He strode along behind all the beasts of the forest — bears, elks, squirrels and hares — who were pouring out, not in chaos, but in orderly groups of their own kind, confident that their master was in charge of his flocks, a heavy whip over his shoulder, and a horn in his hand (Ivanits 1992, p.65).

It is a moving account, with *leshii* depicted as a saviour of the forest, taking all his charges to safety, a giant with compassion for the smallest of creatures. What kind of a vision it was — psychic, literal, or imaginative — we shall never know. Descriptions of nature spirits are probably interpretations, a human way of putting form upon contact with the forces and elements of nature, but they nevertheless do seem to reflect a real degree of experience. And such interpretations always need a cultural context, which provides a kind of visual framework and a repertoire of imagery that makes it easier for people to recount their experiences. Educated, but sensitive, Russians have told me that they too have had experiences of nature spirits.

My own experience in England has mirrored this. Once, on a course that I was taking part in, we investigated the concept of 'elementals', the native spirits of the British tradition that are connected with water, wind, fire and earth. That very afternoon, while we were out for a walk, I nearly tripped over into a fast running river. Perhaps this might seem nothing out of the ordinary, but I definitely had the sense of something playful and downright mischievous tempting me forward, further than I should go, towards the strong current of water. I have treated the idea of nature spirits with respect ever since.

Like most Russian nature spirits, *leshii* has a variety of guises, of which appearing as a giant is only one. He can be seen as a wrinkled old man, wearing a sheepskin coat, with skin gnarled like the bark of the tree; he can turn himself into a mushroom or a blade of grass, or appear as one of the animals or birds he rules over, such as a wolf, bear or raven. He may have soft black fur, or he may be dressed in white. If you want to see him in human form, the best way is to bend over forwards and look backwards through your legs. Reversals of the normal order of the world are common practice if you wish to see into the magical realms, and putting on clothing back to front or harnessing a horse the wrong way round can achieve the same effect. You may hear *leshii* moving around the forest, even if you do not see him, for a rustling of leaves, distant laughter or the whistling of the wind, can all be signs that *leshii* is abroad. He is sometimes said to live in a hole in the tree, sometimes in a well-built wooden house just like those in the villages. His dwelling place is hard to find, though, as it may be surrounded by an impenetrable thicket or a deep bog.

Although *leshii* is unfailingly kind to forest creatures, he is of uncertain temperament where humans are concerned. Whistling in the forest offends him, he will lead you astray in it if he feels so inclined, and you must never stay the night in the forest without asking *leshii*'s permission, or you won't find your way out again the following morning. Dealing with *leshi* could be tricky for country people who grazed their cattle in forest clearings, as *leshii* might take possession of their beasts, so they would try to win his favour by making offerings of eggs and pancakes to him. His habits are worse than that, however, as he may steal babies left on their own, and lure children picking berries or mushrooms on the edge of the forest into its depths until they become hopelessly lost.

Each forest has its own *leshii,* and a *leshii* may have a wife, known as *lesovikha,* and children. *Lesovikha* is not a pretty sight to human eyes, as she usually takes the form of a gigantic woman with huge dangling breasts. Neighbouring forest masters may fall out with one another too, and one folktale relates how two of them quarrelled bitterly over an inheritance. Gambling is another popular pursuit of *leshii,* and, in 1859, peasants attributed an exodus of squirrels across the Ural Mountains to this cause, declaring that one *leshii* was paying off his debts to another after losing at cards, by handing over some of his own creatures to his rival.

Leshii as prankster, gambler, trickster, and saviour — how are we to reconcile all these different images? Like all the nature spirits, his form is fluid, his presence is open to a wide variety of interpretations. Yet at the end of all the varied accounts, we do retain a strong sense of his role as lord of the forest, ruling over its teeming life there, not bound by normal human rules of decent behaviour, but by the flux of nature, and embodying a spirit that echoes the eeriness of the vast forest and its labyrinthine pathways. Paradoxically, when stories and eye witness accounts clothe *leshii* and indeed other nature spirits in a partially human form, we become all the more sharply aware of them as not-human, representing a force that may be uncertain and unreliable in human terms, but which is in keeping with the primal and elemental forces of nature.

The waters of Russia

If forests are the flesh of Russia, then rivers are its veins. And unlike the generalized nature of the forest, the characteristics of rivers are sharply differentiated, each with its own name and attributes. They bring, too, the promise of travel and discovery. Volga, Neva, Moskva, Don, Klazma, Svir, are all names to conjure with, having songs and scenery associated with them, lakes they flow into, towns and cities they pass *en route*. Throughout much of Russia's history, they were its highways, the main roads of the country, and, from early days, provided a route from the Baltic to the Black Sea, known as 'the way from the Varangians (Vikings) to the Greeks'. Boats could travel from Byzantium to Scandinavia this way, and where rivers did not quite meet up, boats could be hauled a few miles overland across a track paved with wooden rollers and brushwood, a system known as 'portage'.

Locally, rivers made a huge difference, allowing visitors and traders to arrive from far-off parts. Settlements would be planned in fact so that they were placed on the bank of navigable river networks, and because of their riverside location, they often grew and became significant trading centres. The current day artists' village of Kholui began life as a humble settlement in about the thirteenth century, when monks fleeing from the Tartar-Mongol invasion are thought to have set up home there and founded a colony to produce icon paintings. The broad river Teza, which flows through the village, is an excellent waterway, connecting as it does with the even mightier Klazma and ultimately with the river Moskva. The village exceeded its initial brief, becoming famous not only for its icons but for its frequent and extensive fairs, which were held there around five times a year. A vast array of goods were traded, not only icons, but items both exotic and homely: furs, vases, shirts, knives, rakes, ribbons, beads, perfumes, books, onions, dried fish and woodcuts. To buy and sell, merchants would arrive from as far away as Turkey and Poland.

Kholui is now an active centre for the painting of Russian lacquer miniatures, but its days of international trade have declined along with the use of the regional network of Russian waterways for transport. As a village, it is tranquil and rarely visited by outsiders. However, traces of the great fairs it once hosted can still be found, and some even turned up in the garden of the wooden house that I owned there. During the periods that I wasn't visiting the house, it was looked after by a cheerful family in the village, who, having five children, were keen to make use of the spacious kitchen garden where they grew potatoes each summer. While planting these, they regularly turned up coins dating from as early as the eighteenth century, and eldest son and art student Misha was so inspired that he began his own museum collection of old village artefacts. The coins were dropped there by merchants or fair goers, because my house stood on land formerly occupied by the fairs, which often had over a hundred booths, and spread widely over the village. Father of the potato planting team, Viktor, painted a superb miniature called 'Kholui Fair', based on research he had done, both from written and oral accounts of the last Kholui Fairs. These continued until the 1930s, when they were suppressed under the Stalinist regime. Up till then, people had a good time at these fairs, such a good time that trading came to a halt around 2pm each afternoon, by which time, it was said, everyone was too drunk to continue!

Or perhaps not quite everyone had such a good time at the fair. A short distance from my house, tucked away in a little grassy clearing at the edge of the village, was a pool, cold and deep. I was told that the depth of this could not be fathomed, that a measuring line had been dropped to 90 metres and had still not touched bottom. In this flat, marshy area, such a depth did not seem possible, but I then learnt that this is thought to be an old salt mine, a commodity produced in Kholui in earlier centuries. I swam in its waters once, and it was chilling both in temperature and atmosphere, especially when I learnt its name.

'We call it Turk's Pool,' a friendly neighbour told me.

'Oh? Why is that?' I asked.

'The story goes that a Turkish merchant arrived at the fair in Kholui and fell out with another local merchant. They quarrelled, the Turk was murdered and dropped into the water here.' He shrugged, cheerfully.

Local waters, then, tell tales of far off lands in Russia, of exotic people and goods, of wealth flowing through villages and towns along the rivers in the form of expensive cargo, and rich buyers who stockpile goods for a lifestyle unknown among the inhabitants, who merely enjoy the spectacle of the fair, and drink to its success. The rivers of Russia must once have been a great source of cultural exchange, as the Silk Road was between China, Central Asia and the Middle East. Stories, many of them tall, would have been traded along with the goods, and the Russian tradition of myth and magic enriched with contributions from neighbouring peoples and beyond.

Even today, when most local rivers are neglected in terms of shipping — the weir at Kholui lies in a state of dilapidation, and the river goes undredged, so that no more sizeable boats can pass through — the major rivers are still significant in the life of the country. They carry freight in large quantities, and are frequented by small-scale cruise ships, offering passengers the chance to see the Russian landscape from the water. The river journeys, which also pass through lakes and along man-made waterways such as the Moscow Ship Canal, are not only worthwhile for the beautiful landscapes and historic towns en route, but also for conveying a sense of the traditional way of travel in Russia, a link with its ancient past.

Vodyanoi, Lord of the Rivers

Just as each forest has its forest master, or *leshii,* so each river has its *vodyanoi,* or lord of the waters. *Vodyanoi* is as powerful and wilful as *leshii,* but more malicious in that his chief aim is to capsize boats and drown swimmers. He lives in deep pools and comes out onto the bank from time to time, to inspect his herds of black cattle, of which he is inordinately fond. *Vodyanoi* can appear in various forms, but is seen most commonly as a tall man, with a dark face, a blue body, greenish hair that flows in long locks, and eyes glowing like coals. 'How the eyes of the water devil glow!' exclaimed one peasant, who escaped from the clutches of *vodyanoi* after falling into the river in the dark. Although *vodyanoi* is antagonistic to humans, he is fond of the company of other underwater spirits. When the river becomes choppy, it means that *vodyanoi's* guests are making merry, drinking and dancing below at an underwater wedding. A standing wave running along the river means that *vodyanoi* himself is setting off in his carriage to join a social gathering

Life above the surface of the river is thus mirrored by the life that occurs below it, in the depths of the water. Some say that the *vodyanoi* lives in a magnificent underwater palace made of crystal, and illuminated by a mysterious light. If you sit by the river on a lazy summer afternoon, and gaze at the reflection of the slender towers and cupolas of the church standing on the bank opposite, they do indeed seem to be the pinnacles and spires of fairyland appearing in the waters below, and perhaps this is one way in which people began to visualize the abode of *vodyanoi.* But later accounts of *vodyanoi* relegate him merely to the muddy depths, with no special dwelling place, and he became thought of more as a water devil rather than a proud regent of the waters.

Although feared by most people, *vodyanoi* was said to have a special relationship with millers and fishermen, who were in one sense his colleagues, even though they still needed to keep on good terms with him by making offerings of bread, salt and tobacco. A more sinister rumour prevailed, however, that the miller would sacrifice a drunkard to *vodyanoi* each year, by drowning him in the mill race to placate the lord of the waters. Fishermen had good reason to keep on the right side of *vodyanoi* too, or else he might tear their nets and hide the fish they had caught; they were, after all, plundering *vodyanoi's* own domain, for, like *leshii* in the forest, he had sovereignty over all the creatures of the water. As the miller took only water from the river, he was on more gracious terms with *vodyanoi,* and would sometimes even be invited to dine with him in his underwater mansion.

Vodyanoi may drown those who enter his waters, and there are indeed many incidents of people drowning in the rivers of Russia. Roma, a young man of my acquaintance, drowned in the waters of the Teza as he returned home late one evening to his house in Kholui. This river, which looks so placid in summer, studded with yellow water lilies, with small boats drifting on its surface, and children splashing happily in the shallows, becomes a monster each spring as the snows melt and swell the waters. The village is flooded regularly; people are prepared for this, and rather enjoy the experience, with waders and boats ready to hand, even if they do have to raise the furniture up off the floor while the flood waters rise. But the floods also often sweep away the one road bridge over the river which joins the two sides of the village, and, when this happens, a temporary wooden bridge is usually put up a short distance away. Roma may have missed his footing as he tried to cross the sketchily made new bridge in the dark; he fell into the raging river, and his body was not found for weeks. It is a reminder that stories about nature spirits are founded on real experience of the elemental forces in Russia.

Frogs and fishes

Once upon a time, there were three brothers, three bachelor princes who had not yet found themselves brides, and their parents were tired of them hanging around at home.

'Go outside, and each of you shoot off an arrow,' they commanded their idle sons. 'Follow the flight of the arrow, and where it comes down to earth, there you will find a lovely girl waiting for you.'

The brothers shot off their arrows as instructed. The first two did indeed find beautiful brides clutching the arrows that they had aimed at random into the air. But the third, Prince Ivan, found only a little frog holding his arrow, and he was mightily dismayed. This was not the girl of his dreams.

'Give me back my arrow,' he told her.

'I will, on one condition,' she said.

'Oh, and what's that?' the prince asked the frog scornfully, in a tone suitable for addressing such a lowly creature of ponds and muddy places.

'That you marry me,' she said. Ivan was forced to obey her. But the frog, of course, was no frog at all, but a princess who had been bewitched into this shape. Ivan kept his word and stood by her, and after many trials and tribulations, the princess was returned to her former beautiful self, and the couple lived happily ever after.

This fairy story of *The Frog Princess* is well-known in Russia, and carries the message that watery creatures may not always be what they seem, a theme which is echoed elsewhere.

> 'Let me go free, and I will be of use to you,' pleads a pike, which a young hero, our second Prince Ivan, has caught in the waters. 'What use could you possibly be to me?' Ivan asks the fish. 'The impossible is sometimes possible,' replies the pike.[3]

And so it proves to be. Magic fish that grant wishes turn up quite often in Russian wonder tales, the best-known of these being Emelya and the Magic Pike (see Fig. 28). Here, the youngest brother of a family, considered to be its ugliest and most stupid member, catches a pike through a hole in the ice. The pike offers to be of assistance in all future matters, if Emelya promises to spare its life. All he has to do is to utter the words: 'By the will of the pike, do as I like!' and matters will rearrange themselves accordingly. By this means, his kitchen stove is turned into a flying machine, and he is also transformed into a handsome and clever youth, fit to marry the princess who he has fallen in love with.

Fools are not mere fools in the Russian tradition. They win through because of their lack of pretension and steadfastness; as one source puts it: 'The fool as depicted in Russian folk-tales is not a fool at all. He is a simple-hearted, kind, and compassionate person who knows his own value and cares very little about the others' opinion of him' (Krasunov 1996, p.172). Fools are wise, too, when it comes to the spirits of nature, who may be tricky to deal with, but these spirits respect those who keep their word and may grant extraordinary gifts and blessings in return. After our previous hero, the second Prince Ivan, releases his pike back into the waters, the pike returns to him one day, carrying an egg in its mouth. In the egg lies the death of Koshchei, and from Koshchei's death, Ivan is able to win the beautiful Princess Iakuta.[4] The pike is returning the favour: 'Remember that a debt repaid is beautiful,' he reminds the young prince.

Perhaps, then, our seemingly amoral and cantankerous nature spirits are a source of a different kind of ethics, ones which rest on genuine behaviour and integrity. Those people who are humble may more readily become attuned to the forces of nature, and not only survive in this enchanted landscape, but be blessed by it. Those, on the other hand, who consider themselves superior, and despise lowly forms of nature, such as the ugly pike and the slimy frog, those who consider that they can conquer wind and water, fire and earth, may be in for a shock, because they cannot ultimately defeat the elements, and their pride may bring about their own downfall.

In Pushkin's literary fairy tale, *The Tale of the Fisherman and the Golden Fish,* based on traditional themes, the golden fish likewise promises wishes aplenty to the old man who has caught it, if he releases the fish back into the waters. The old fellow returns to his wife, who starts to demand various improvements in her lot, beginning with a humble request to replace her cracked washing trough, and culminating with a wish to become a queen in her own palace. All she asks for is granted, but when she makes a final demand to be mistress of the rivers and seas, her wealth and status vanish in an instant, and she finds herself back in the old cottage again, poor and helpless once more, with a cracked wash trough standing in front of her. She may have anything but this; the waters are not hers to rule.

Mermaids

Russian mermaids are somewhat different from our Western mermaids. A *rusalka* as she is known, (plural *rusalki*), lives in rivers and pools rather than in the sea, and she is equally at home roaming around in the forest too. 'A mermaid sits in the branches,' the poet Pushkin declaims, in his famous Prologue to *Ruslan and Ludmilla,* in which he imagines himself sitting under a mighty oak tree, listening to Russian stories and watching the characters from these who pass like a vision before his eyes. It is Pushkin's homage to the Russian tradition that inspired so much of his work, and he concludes with the words: 'There is a Russian odour there — it smells of Russia! And I was there, I drank mead ... I remember one (story), and this story I will now tell to the world.'

The mermaid who he describes may have left her watery home, as *rusalki* are wont to do, during their own week's festival, which is known as *Rusal'naia,* and attached to the holiday of Trinity Sunday (Whitsun). *Rusalki* are usually seen as young and beautiful girls, with slim legs rather than tails such as Western mermaids have, and they are often dressed in white robes, with garlands of flowers set in their locks of flowing light brown hair. But they are dangerous. They prowl the forest to look for humans to lure into the water's depths, especially handsome young men who will make good lovers. One method they employ is to call out men's names at random, such as 'Sasha!' 'Dima!' 'Kolya!' Sooner or later, some man of that name will answer, and, when he does, he becomes their captive, and is doomed to live with them underwater in lake or river.

Mermaids are elusive creatures, like other nature spirits, and there is no complete agreement between scholars as to what they represent; although usually seen as lovely girls, they can also appear as ugly old hags, and they may be either spirits of nature who are the welcome bringers of fertility and moisture to the land, or else they may be portrayed as the lost souls of human girls who had drowned, usually before they were married.[5] One folk narrative tells the story of Marina, a young woman who had fallen in love with a man called Ivan Kurhcavyi, who overlooked her, however, and got married to another girl. Marina drowned herself in the Volga in despair, and thus became a *rusalka.* But ultimately Ivan chose to leave his wife and join Marina in her home at the bottom of a whirlpool, where he was apparently very happy, and even played dance tunes for the *vodyanoi* who lived in that particular spot (Ivanits 1992, pp.188–9).

The waters of life and death

Rivers, springs and wells have long been venerated in Russian culture; many of them are considered to be sacred or to have healing properties, and offerings to them are made in the form of a coin tossed into the depths, or a rag or ribbon tied to a branch nearby, placed there along with a prayer for the restoration of health or wellbeing. Springs or pools have often been associated with St Paraskeva, the Christian saint who has a close affinity with the Russian mother goddess, as we have seen in Chapter 2. Even in the nineteenth century, her devout followers would throw a piece of bread into her waters, while asking for healing.

Another kind of magical waters in Russian myth are not found in the familiar landscape, however, but in the mysterious otherworld, the realm of the thrice-ten kingdom, beyond the thrice-nine land. The Waters of Life and Death are potions which are sought in many a Russian fairytale, and they are the ultimate restorative. It is these waters which Grey Wolf sends the raven to find in the story of *Prince Ivan and the Grey Wolf,* in order to bring Ivan back to life again, as we saw in Chapter 4. Worship of sacred wells and springs is common to many, if not most, countries, but the Waters of Life and Death are concepts which are uniquely Slavic (see Phillips & Kerrigan 1999, p.49). There are two separate kinds of water: the Waters of Death which heal the wounds of a dead body, or, as in Ivan's case, puts back together again its dismembered parts; and the Waters of Life which restore the presence of life itself to the corpse. It is no easy thing to obtain these Waters, which may be protected by fierce guardians such as Baba Yaga or Koshchei the Deathless, for a special effort is needed to find them, and only the very determined or heroic can achieve this, unless a magical creature such as Grey Wolf steps into the breach to help out. For these spirit helpers it can be easy — in one rather more prosaic story, Mishka the bear pops out to the shops to buy two pints of living water for the hero to sprinkle on his dead brother. *(The Serpent Slayer* in Haney 2001, vol. I, p.7.)

The magical landscape

I have chosen to focus on forest and water in this chapter as the two chief elements in the Russian landscape, ones which play a major part in both traditional and modern life, and which generate a multitude of tales of nature spirits, and magical encounters. I myself have found the landscape enchanted, and what I have endeavoured to do here is to convey its essence, both in terms of myth and of natural beauty, revealing some of the deep, age-old lore about nature that has been handed down through the generations. Even if we do not believe literally in all the stories of spirits associated with it, reflecting upon them can put us in touch with the landscape in a more direct way, and help us to become more sensitive to its elemental powers.

7

The Wheel of Time

> The Russian folk calendar is an extraordinarily interesting phenomenon. Unfortunately, it is little known to the reading public at large. Yet it is a part of the history of the Russian people, and of their culture. Getting to know the folk calendar will help you to open up a bright new chapter of traditional culture and the sources of national spirituality, and to get a better idea of the Russian national character and type. (Rozhnova 1992, p.5)

So begins a remarkable little book, *The Russian Folk Calendar,* largely unknown in its English translation, but a resource which has proved a godsend to me in many of my research projects over the years. Entries covering every month of the year, and many of their specific days, cite activities involving divination, weather lore, folk rituals, farming traditions, household customs, and observances relating to Christian saints, pagan deities and nature spirits. The folk calendar thus provides the framework for the year, and spells out the rhythm of daily life, in which magical and mundane are inextricably linked.

Calendars have prime importance in human life, and are deeply embedded in our cultures. There are over forty different types of calendars in use in the world today, each dividing up time into units in its own way, all relying on cycles for their structure; the Western calendar for instance, is based on the cycle of the sun, whereas the Islamic calendar works on lunar cycles. The current calendar used in Russia is the Gregorian calendar, the same as the Western calendar that is used on an international basis now. It was adopted after the October Revolution in 1917, when newly-liberated Russian citizens were advised that Wednesday,

January 31, 1918, was to be followed immediately by Thursday, February 14, 1918.[1] But the older Julian calendar which preceded it is still used by the Russian Orthodox Church, and is apparent in some of the customs celebrated in the folk calendar, so that 'old' Christmas begins on the eve of January 6, for instance.

Although the Russian folk calendar contains many dates linked to the feast days of the church and its saints, it is also bound closely to the astronomical cycle, and the cycle of nature. The solstices, the shortest and longest days of the year, are of prime importance, as are the equinoxes, when days and nights are of equal length. These are the marking points of the year, its cardinal points in terms of the sun's progress, and of the balance between darkness and light. As we saw earlier, the symbol of a 'rolling' sun, travelling in its circle around the sky, is prominent in Russian folk tradition, and is found in many of its symbols and rituals, from the eating of pancakes in spring, to the embroidery of 'walking suns' on ceremonial towels.

Our concept of time in modern society is mainly linear, but we are heavily dependent nevertheless upon the kind of cyclical time that calendars embody, with the days of the week and the months of the year succeeding each other, and then returning again. We may think about life as a progression from past to future, but we depend upon the recurrence of 'Monday', or 'December', both to organize the structure of our lives, and to recognize the repeating patterns of the seasons. Without acknowledging cycles of time in some form, we would not only struggle to function, but we would also be culturally impoverished, for months and days build up their own set of meanings. This is something that lies so close to home that we often ignore it, but is worth examining here in order to see its significance. The Russian folk calendar makes this cycle of time much more apparent; it uses the months of the standard, official calendar, but is far richer in events and rituals, which are attuned both to agriculture and to cosmology, and traditions that are spiritual as well as practical. As a wheel of time, the folk calendar is also bound up with practices of divination and magic. It is commonly believed in traditional cultures that there are certain times of the year when the veil between the human and spirit world is especially thin, and at these points, the otherworld may be penetrated by ritual and scrying — familiar examples in the West are Hallowe'en, and the Twelve Days of Christmas. The gods or spirits can be contacted, and may choose to reveal what is in store for us. This divinatory aspect of the calendar is very prominent in Russian folk practices, as will be seen in examples given below.

The calendar is by definition a fixed framework, but it has fluidity in terms of the observances that it contains. The Russian folk calendar already contends with the two different dating systems, old and new, and it has evolved over the centuries to produce imaginative syntheses that combine the feast days of Christian saints with indigenous deities and their rites. Within its compass, too, some traditions die out over time, and others are adopted. Likewise, there may be regional variations, so that in different localities, certain customs contained in the folk calendar are well-known all over Russia, whereas others may be unfamiliar outside their area. It is with this in mind that we should look at any transcribed versions of the Russian folk calendar, including the excellent version produced by Rozhnova. A folk calendar is, in effect, a myth in its own right, laying out a combination of traditions practised in different regions at any one time, and/or a composite of calendar customs that have come and gone over the years. There is probably no golden age of the Russian folk calendar, and the chances are that it has always been in a continual state of adaptation. But it remains as a testimony to the traditions of the country, many of which are still practised today, and, as such, is recognized as part of the Russian heritage, and as an element of Russian culture in general.

New challenges to the calendar arise too in today's world, with its multicultural societies. In 2006, I visited Uzbekistan, a former colony of the Soviet Empire, now independent, but retaining a strong Russian influence and its own community of Russians. The staff in the hotel where we were staying in Tashkent had worked out that it was Easter in the western Christian Church, and kindly set up a breakfast buffet in our honour full of the dishes that Russians celebrate Easter with — coloured hard-boiled eggs, *kulich* cake (tall, sponge-like and a little dry) and sweetened curd cheese. British people on the tour who hadn't come across Russian

Easter customs before were bemused by the spread, and opted for more familiar dishes on offer. And any Russian guests staying at the hotel were puzzled, because Orthodox Easter comes later for them, and they were still only at the stage of Palm Sunday. When we went out that day, we saw local Russians carrying branches of pussy willow to church, as is the custom for this festival (see Chapter 6, p.132). The local Uzbeks, on the other hand, had no Islamic observance that day, and went about their business as usual, indifferent to the other two festivals being celebrated.

The year turns

Just about every other day in the Russian folk calendar has a special tradition or feast day associated with it. As mentioned above, many are dedicated to a being who is an amalgamation of a native deity with a Christian saint, resulting in some very idiosyncratic characters. To give an idea of their richness and variety, a selection of customs follows, one chosen out of the listings for each month of the year:

January 4

St Anastasia's day, the saint who safeguards pregnant women. She is known as 'the safe cutter of umbilical cords', and her day was traditionally celebrated in honour of the family and the mother. For safe delivery, a woman should have ready a linen towel embroidered with magical symbols, such as diamonds, to ward off the evil eye, and this towel must be finished by January 4 in order to benefit from Anastasia's protection. The midwife at the delivery wipes both mother and child with this towel, thus cleansing them from all negative influences, and bringing peace into their lives.

February 10

This is *domavoi's* birthday. The mischievous house spirit, whom we have already met on several occasions, must be honoured with a special meal to keep him in a good temper. Otherwise he may overturn buckets of water, knock down piles of firewood, and generally create chaos in the home. For his birthday treat, a pot of porridge, preferably made of millet and with a nice skin of milk on the top, will go down very well. Failing that, oat porridge with butter is also acceptable.

March 9

Dedicated to the birds, which are said to start building their nests on this day. Russians are fond of birds, and traditionally bird boxes for starlings are put up at this time, as starlings are considered rather exotic in Russia. The word for bird houses is *skvorechnika* after the word for starling, *skvorets.* It is also a day when divination can be practised by observing the behaviour of birds: if they are returning early from their winter migration, then there will be a good grain harvest, and if they are building their nests on the sunny side of trees or houses, then the summer will be cool.

April 14

A day that belongs to St Mary the Egyptian, whose popular name is Mary the Snowmelter. She is a spirit associated with fire and warmth, and she now melts the snow, sends sunbeams playing over the land, and invites young girls outside to play spring games. If she manages to thaw the ice easily, then the year too will be happy and easy.

May 27

St Isidore's day, a saint known as Sidor the Cucumber Man. Under his influence, cucumbers can now be planted, and a clear day on Sidor's day brings a good crop in due course. It is also the day when the swallows are expected to return, bringing fair weather with them if they fly high.

June 14

The day of fences, presided over by St Justin. No one was supposed to put up fences on this day, although an exception was made for a maiden who wanted to rid herself of an unwelcome suitor. She was advised to cut a branch of willow, and push it into the ground between them, thus fencing him off from her, and generating enough magic to keep him away permanently.

July 1

A day known as 'the crest of summer', the time when the forces of the season are at their peak. Curiously enough, the climax of summer is traditionally used for a more macabre and shadowy form of divination. People weave wreaths from birch trees, which must be finished before noon. They then repair to the river, where they stand on a bank just above the water's surface, and gaze at the water through the wreath; there they will see reflected all the faces of their loved ones who had been killed in foreign wars.

August 19

Often known as Apple Day. In Christian terms, it is an important festival, the Transfiguration of the Saviour, but in popular culture it gives licence to start eating apples — strictly speaking, no one should eat an apple off the tree until now. It was on this day, in my house in Kholui, that Viktor the caretaker burst in, already a little the worse for wear, and insisting that we should drink with him to celebrate the new apple season. Since we had all been eating apples well before this date anyway, his rationale was that we should mark the day in another time-honoured way, with a toast or two.

Those still sober should watch out for weather signs too on this day — a clear day betokens a sharp winter, and a northerly wind indicates a good time to plant rye.

September 13

A day of wistful farewells, marking the departure of the cranes from the land in the folk calendar. Children run through the fields that have been harvested, calling out to the cranes as they fly away, 'May your journey be like a wheel!' in the belief that the cranes will thus be encouraged to come back the following year. It was also once believed that on this day the cranes held a kind of sports rally in the marshes before taking off for warmer climes, testing each other's wingspan, strength, and eyesight, so as to elect a leader for the flight.

October 2

Dedicated to St Zosima, who is the Defender of Bees. This signifies that it is time to bring in the hives for the winter, and people are recommended to eat a teaspoonful of honey each morning for nine days after this festival, to strengthen them for the rigours of the cold weather ahead. The behaviour of bees is also studied, to predict the severity or mildness of the winter to come.

November 8

A day to remember the dead, under the patronage of St Demetrius. The Saturday before this day is particularly significant, and known as Parents' Saturday, when it is the custom to remember and honour one's parents. Traditionally, people would also visit graveyards and eat a feast for the dear departed, which consisted of bread, soup, salt, cakes and pancakes. The first pancake taken out of the basket should be spread with butter and honey, as a symbol of sweetness and eternity.

December 13

St Andrew's day, in times past given over more to divination than worship. Girls would be up early, eager to tell their fortunes. They would hurry outside to look for tracks in the snow, which would give them a clue as to their future luck, depending on what kind of person or creature had made them. Other people made a hole through the ice in the frozen river, and knelt down to listen to what was going on below. Noisy water meant blizzards and sharp frosts to come, whereas a more peaceful flow of water foretold an easier winter.

Four festivals

Marking the calendar are a number of major festivals, whose popularity and significance have fluctuated through the centuries. The four I have selected here are not equally spaced through the year, but they each have their own character, and are rich in folklore and symbolism. Two are popular at the current time, and two have passed more into the realm of heritage, though they may also still be practised to a certain degree. With these festivals, we move around the circle of time, and bring this exploration of Russian mythology and magic to a full close, ending, as we began, with the great oak tree, the mythic Tree of Life.

Maslnitsa

Moscow, 2002: It is a cold, cheerless day in February, in the park of Kolomonskoe on the outskirts of the city. There should be snow on the ground, but winter has been doing strange things in Russia of late, and the earth is bare and damp; earlier frost and snow killed the last crop of grass, and now, an unseasonable thaw has exposed the ground again, on which it is much too early for new growth to appear. It is still winter, but people are here to celebrate the very first hints of spring in an ancient festival called Maslnitsa. Maslnitsa is now tied to the Church calendar, and is the equivalent of the week prior to Lent, the last days of celebrations and good eating before the period of fasting and solemnity sets in. Self-denial is certainly yet to come, for the name Maslnitsa comes from the word for fat, butter or oil, and it is a time for feasting and rejoicing. Traditionally, games are played in the snow — races on sledges and in sleighs, sliding down artificially created ice slopes, and, in Siberia, a popular team game called 'Storming the Snow Fortress'. For this, a castle is made with bricks of snow, and one team tries to take the fortress, while the other defends it.

In Moscow, although there is a lack of snow, the celebration is on a large scale, and crowds have turned up to enjoy Maslnitsa at Kolomonskoe. Walking through the lower stretches of the park and on up the hill, towards the old church and palace on its summit, I come across various groups, some trying their luck at fairground booths, and others dressed in traditional costume, kicking up their heels to folk melodies as they dance in a circle. In the church porch, I find two young men playing the *gusli,* the instrument of old Russia and its bards, and beyond them, a merry trio consisting of two stout old ladies and one old man sitting between them, playing the *garmon'*, the small Russian accordion. They are all singing their heads off (see Fig. 16). At the food stalls, pancakes are on the menu, for this is the feast of the Sun god, and you can buy a souvenir of Yarilo, the Sun god himself, in the form of a golden raffia sun wearing a cheerful smile and adorned with orange flames.

A little while later, the door of one of the old buildings housed in the park bursts open, and a procession emerges carrying the giant size doll, the Maslnitsa effigy, who is dressed as a woman.

Later in the day, she must be ritually destroyed, thrown on a bonfire to hasten the arrival of spring. Everyone sings to her, and her attendants dance around her as she is conveyed towards the place where she will finally meet her fate (see Fig. 9).

In the wide open spaces down below, now muddy from all the trampling feet, a band is playing on a makeshift stage, a folk ensemble generating lively tunes that get everybody going. Mothers, children, young men, grandparents, all form a human chain and dance along together, weaving a long line through bystanders and market stalls, and jigging to the irresistible rhythm as they go. Later, there will be a full-scale concert here, mirroring other Maslnitsa celebrations in the city. It is a day to remember, and to return to next year; Maslnitsa is enjoying a full-scale revival in Russia, and has survived the transition from village to urban environment. Other signs of it have appeared in the city; restaurants in the capital have been serving creative variations on the traditional pancakes for the whole week, and huge cut-out Maslnitsa dolls decorate the craft market of Izmailovo. It is a calendar festival that seems well set to continue indefinitely into the future (see Fig. 17).

Troitsa: Trinity Sunday

The birch tree comes into its own at the summer festival of Troitsa, which is usually held in June. This festival spans both an ancient festival to welcome summer, and the Feast of Pentecost of the Orthodox Church (Whitsun), which takes place on the seventh Sunday after Easter. Trinity Sunday was originally a part of *Rusal'naia,* the week when mermaids leave their watery homes, and walk abroad through the forest, as described in the previous chapter. The main focus of the festival, however, is to celebrate the new green growth, and the birch is the tree chosen to represent this in both sacred and secular surroundings. Branches of birch, and even whole saplings, are brought into church and displayed there, and switches of birch may be blessed at the Whitsun service and taken home to be placed by the family icon, in the same way that pussy willow twigs are on Palm Sunday. In 2004, visiting the northern port of Murmansk, I saw a potted birch tree placed by the altar of a small Orthodox church, which had been newly built there; even though the month was June and the days were long, not a great deal grows at this latitude and people struggle even to cultivate the basic Russian staple of the potato. Nevertheless, summer was celebrated in the form of a living tree, along with the religious rites to mark the Christian feast day.

In village context, the prime ritual was once carried out by young girls, who chose a birch tree in the forest to decorate and revere. They tied ribbons to its branches, and circled around it, singing:

Oh birch so curly,
Curly and young ...
Under you, little birch,
No fire is burning,
No poppy is blooming —
Pretty maids
Are dancing a khorovod,[2]
About you, little birch,
They are singing songs.

The birch tree is chosen above all others at this time:

Don't rejoice oak trees ...
Not to you the girls are coming ...
Rejoice, birches,
Rejoice, green ones!
To you the girls are coming,
To you they are bringing pies,
Pastries, omelettes ...

Sometimes these omelettes would be left under the tree for the whole of *Rusal'naia* week, to feed the mermaids and other nature spirits, as well as to pay homage to the birch.

As they danced around the tree, girls would often ask for blessings for their mothers, sometimes plaiting its branches beforehand in order to bring them good health. They also performed rites of divination to test their luck in love, including the practice of weaving birch garlands and tossing them into the river to see how they floated (see Chapter 5, p. 113). Any young man who stumbled upon their rites, deep in the forest, was in for a ducking in the nearest pond or river, especially since the *khorovod* itself is a form of sacred dance, a female circle that must not be broken by any male intrusion (see Fig. 23). An early twentieth century painting by Andrei Ryabushkin, called *A boy has wormed his way into the khorovod,* shows just that — an enthusiastic lad who cannot resist joining in the girls' dancing, and we can be sure that he will shortly pay the price.

Ivan Kupala: the day of John the Baptist

By the earlier, Julian calendar, the feast day of St John the Baptist falls upon July 7, but it is also considered to be the Midsummer Festival, and can be celebrated as such on June 24. Its symbol is fire, and bonfires are lit for the daring to leap over. The mythical 'flower of fire' is said to bloom then, and anyone brave enough can venture into the forest to search for it, wearing a wreath made of nettles and carrying a twig from a rowan tree for protection. The flower is really a fern, which, according to legend, blossoms on this night only. If you find the flower, you must draw a magic ring around you with the rowan twig, and gaze fearlessly at the blossom, which gives off a heat all of its own. It is important to stay in this magic circle all night, steadfast in spirit, despite the howling of demons who try to penetrate the circle and torment you. At first light, you can search for the treasure which is buried nearby, according to one tradition, or take the flower home with you as a talisman for love and happiness, according to another.

Herbs are considered to be at their most potent at the festival of Ivan Kupala, and wise women, healers, and anyone needing herbs for divination or magical spells will pick them then. The best practice is to say a prayer before picking, such as: 'Mother Earth, grant me your blessing to gather some of your plants.' It is also the time when switches of birch twigs are gathered for the bathhouse, where they are hung upside down from wall or ceiling, tied in neat bundles until they are dried and ready for use. The dew of Ivan Kupala's feast day is also magical, and it has long been the custom to bathe your face in it, to enhance its beauty, remove wrinkles, and even cure illnesses. Women lay a cloth or cotton scarf over the grass to soak up the dew, then wring it out, either using the dew immediately, or storing it in birch bark containers as a future cure or cosmetic. The dew is an omen too: 'Plenty of dew on St John's Day means a good harvest of cucumbers,' as the farmers used to say.

The fire of the midsummer sun, and the waters associated with John the Baptist form a powerful interplay of the elements, the fire and water that are in one sense at war with one another, but whose combination is potent and creative, the basis of transformation, as it is said in the alchemical tradition.[3] These specific customs may have died out to a certain degree, but awareness of the tradition remains, and a recent recording called *Ivan Kupala,* which combines pop and folk music celebrating the festival, has become a best-seller. The Russian film-maker, Andrei Tarkovsky, also paid tribute to Ivan Kupala in his 1966 film, *Andrei Rublev,* a fictional account of the famous icon-painter of the middle ages. While Rublev and his followers are travelling to the monastery town of Vladimir in June, 1408, they stumble across a Kupala celebration on the banks of the Klazma river, a sensual ritual which includes a procession of naked men and women, carrying lighted torches, as they head towards the river to perform the solemn rites there, and then celebrate with sexual embraces. Here, too, the combination of fire and water is marked; as one commentator puts it: 'Fire and water are central to the pagan rituals of St John's Eve [and] they are also central to Tarkovsky's own personal film imagery.'[4]

New Year

'On this day people would come out of their homes to greet the sun and drive away the frost. The custom was to start the day with a bow to your home and your land.'

New Year is probably the chief celebration in the Russian calendar today. Christmas had a stronger place in earlier folk and popular custom than it does now, the church festivals having been played down by Soviet authorities, and New Year lending itself so well to modern festivities. New Year's Eve is commonly celebrated within the family, with perhaps a few honoured guests invited, and a feast laid on during the evening, to be enjoyed at leisure while waiting for the magic hour of midnight to arrive. Everyone should wear something red for luck — red, it may be recalled, is the colour of beauty. The *yolka* or fir tree graces the living room, often ablaze with fairy lights and hung with chocolate treats and glass baubles, just as it is in the West. Traditional songs are sung to the *yolka* and games may be played around it. As midnight approaches, everyone must charge their glasses with vodka, and drink a toast to the New Year: *'S'novim godom!'* 'To the New Year!'

Presiding over the New Year festivities are the magical personages of Father Frost and Snowmaiden. Father Frost we have met already (see Chapter 4, p. 78); *Ded Moroz,* or Grandfather Frost as he is actually known in Russian, is a gigantic, crackling, freezing presence who strides through the forest, carrying a magic staff (see Fig. 27). The best-known story about him concerns a little girl who is abandoned in the forest in the middle of winter on the orders of her cruel stepmother. As she sits on a fallen log, awaiting her fate, a huge hoary face looms out of the branches, and she sees Father Frost looking at her. 'How are you today, my little girl, my beauty?' he asks, as he approaches her, full of curiosity as to what she is doing in the forest on her own. Being a well-behaved young lady, she answers him politely, even though her teeth are chattering. 'I'm very well, thank you, Father Frost,' she replies. When he realizes that she is turning blue and numb because he is standing much too close to her, he retreats, apologizing, and rewards her with all sorts of choice gifts, such as fur coats, velvet wraps, and caskets of jewels, in return for her patience and good manners.

Her stepmother sends the sledge out to the forest to pick up the corpse of her stepdaughter. Finding to her chagrin that the girl is still alive, she grudgingly allows her to come home, but orders her own two girls to be left in the forest so that they too may meet Father Frost, and likewise be endowed with precious gifts. Unfortunately, these two wenches are foul-mouthed, swearing at Father Frost when he approaches, and angering him so much that he decides to freeze them to death. The innocent stepsister, however, catches the eye of a rich prince with her beauty and handsome dowry, and lives happily ever after. This is yet another example of the moral found in Russian fairy tales: respect the elements, and they will treat you well in return. Challenge or annoy them, and they can destroy you.

Father Frost has in recent years become more and more like Father Christmas in Russian celebrations, and I have noticed that the carved wooden models you can buy of him in the craft markets now mostly paint his robe in red, as opposed to the more traditional blue. Like Father Christmas, he has a bushy white beard, and wears a long robe with high boots, but he always carries his special staff, and drives a troika rather than a team of reindeer. Perhaps Father Frost will evolve further as time goes on; it is a good reminder that myths and customs are never totally static.

Snowmaiden is Father Frost's helper in the New Year festivities. They may be pictured together on decorations, or a lissom girl may dress up in Snowmaiden's traditional costume of delicate blue-green, spangled with silver, to help Father Frost hand out presents to children. Like Father Frost, Snowmaiden is a semi-mythic personage, who appears in stories, but who also exists in her own right. Sometimes she is said to be the daughter of Father Frost and Mother Spring, whereas at others, she appears more to be Father Frost's consort. The popular fairy story of *Snowmaiden* describes how an elderly couple make a little girl out of snow to play with, as they can't have children of their own. But the little snow girl comes to life before their very eyes, and stays with them as their daughter. She is beautiful, kind and affectionate, and they could wish for nothing better. However, Snowmaiden falls in love with a shepherd boy called Lel. He likes to play his pipe, and one fine day in spring, he invites her to come outside and dance to his music (see Fig. 7). Alas for Snowmaiden! As she dances under the first rays of the spring sun, she melts away.

But the story is not a tragedy, for Snowmaiden is in her own way immortal; she appears every year with the first flakes of snow, and vanishes again in the spring thaw. She represents, too, the stirrings of love, the warmth inside her own heart which causes her exquisite beauty to melt, and the moral of the story, if there is one, is that love is not to be resisted, even though it can cause the familiar world around us to change beyond recognition. It is necessary to have faith in love, which will bring renewal in its own time; with no thaw, the snows would become dirty and the land could not turn green again. Next winter's snows will be all the more beautiful and pristine because of the changing seasons.

A final symbol of New Year brings us back once more to the oak tree, the Tree of Life which we might call the essence and core of Russian mythology. New Year is a time for divination, and for invoking a vision of the year ahead. In times gone by, people would visualize this year ahead of them on the evening of December 31 as an oak tree with twelve nests in its branches, one for every month of the year. Each nest contains four eggs, representing the four weeks of the month, and each egg has seven chicks inside it, waiting to hatch out as the days of the week. Days, weeks and months form the progress of the year, beautifully envisaged in this ancient symbol. Every New Year is a step forward, its joys and sorrows as yet unknown, but the calendar and its rituals help to mark that way forward, to keep faith with old traditions and the spirit of the Russian people in their land.

Epilogue: The Soul of Russia, Today and Tomorrow

I stepped out of the metro station in Moscow on an icy January evening. It was already dark, and I found myself lost amidst a forest of apartment blocks, dotted apparently at random over an uninspiring stretch of snowy wastes and half-cleared paths. I looked at the address I had written down, and wondered if I was ever going to find it. Who could I ask? Hundreds of people were still pouring out of the metro, eager to get back to a warm and well-lit home after a day at work. But they were all striding purposefully in their chosen directions, and I hesitated to ask anyone for help; few could manage any English, and in the early 1990s, I had not yet learnt to speak much Russian.

Finally, I plucked up my courage and asked an attractive young woman if she knew where this address was.

'Oh,' she said, speaking in excellent English, 'are you going to the alchemy lecture too?'

'Well, yes,' I said. 'In fact, I'm giving it.'

Laughing, she introduced herself as Marina, and led me confidently to the right tower block. We went up in its creaky lift to the small apartment where the talk was to be given to a gathering of twenty or so people, all with an interest in astrology and keen to learn how it related to alchemy, the magical art of making gold.

My first response to this coincidence was to exclaim how extraordinary it was that I picked one of the very few people out of the crowd who were going to participate in this event. But perhaps the happenstance was a symptom of something occurring on a greater scale. My talk on alchemy, not a world-shattering event in its own right, was nevertheless a manifestation of the incredible surge of energy and interest that arose from the new encounter between Russia and the West at this time. The meeting was one small spark from that surge, and perhaps the power of this contact carried its own element of destiny, making it almost inevitable that I *did* meet Marina, the young woman, outside the metro that evening. It was as if we had stepped into a realm where the energy was so powerful that it could sometimes override the normal laws of chance and coincidence. All kinds of interactions were now occurring on a personal level as well as on the global stage, and the sum total of these was changing the world forever.

Russia old and new

In the twenty-first century, Russia is now no longer insulated from the rest of the world. Over seventy years of Communism effectively sealed its borders, preventing easy contact with other nations and their influences. Of course, this was not an absolute isolation, but there were strong barriers in place which allowed only a trickle of ideas, news and fashion to seep through. In the late 1970s I met some Russian astrophysicists at a party held by a friend of mine in Cambridge, and I remember gazing at them with fascination, as though they were an exotic species. They were probably the first Russians I had ever set eyes on, and their taciturn presence meant that they remained an enigma to me.

There was virtually no commerce between Russia and the West, and in the 1980s I was astonished to be able to buy two sturdy wooden desks for my children at my local furniture store which were made in Russia. (They are still intact, a testimony to the strength, if not the elegance, of Russian manufacture.) All trading was conducted through strictly controlled channels. When I first began to buy crafts in Russia at the beginning of the 1990s, I met some representatives of the former government trade delegations, the old, brown-suited, chain smoking officials, still trying to hold on to their position, which was fast being eroded. Until recently, their word had governed all buying and selling activity with foreigners, but now, as their power waned swiftly, they were keen to offer to arrange exhibitions abroad by top artists and craftsmen, in order to have one last chance of an all-expenses paid trip abroad.

The normal exchange of trade and barter had been absent from Russia from a generation, and, as is known from the history of the

Silk Road, merchants convey not only goods, but culture, religion and art from one country to another (see Gilchrist 1999: *Stories from the Silk Road).* Without open trading, Russia had lost the opportunity to share news and views with the world. Stagnation was inevitable, although this exclusion did also help to preserve much of the traditional way of life and the native belief system that I have explored in this book.

Once those barriers went down after the fall of the Soviet Empire, a tidal wave of new ideas and influences poured into the country and to its former satellite states. It was common, for instance, to find your hotel in Moscow or St Petersburg overrun with a Baptist mission from the United States, whose members would commandeer the dining room for hymn singing between meals. The Salvation Army set up charitable soup kitchens and refuges in the cities, and all kinds of psychical, spiritualist and esoteric movements, from Hare Krishna to The Great White Brotherhood, tried to gain a foothold in this new territory. Reactions set in; it wasn't long, for instance, before the government introduced restrictions on 'non-Russian' religious activity. When a broad-based study organization, of which I was a member, offered to host seminars in Moscow on philosophy and mythology in 1994, we were met at first with a blank policy of non-communication, despite having friendly links with some of the people in the corresponding Russian group. It took some time before we realized that they had been inundated with such offers from the West, and were wary of inviting foreigners who might be attempting a new form of brainwashing. They had had enough of being imposed on by those who thought they knew better under the old Communist regime. It also took a little time before they decided that they could trust us, and we began a series of seminars that turned out to be a valuable exchange of knowledge for all of us, especially in comparing the ancient myths of Russia and of Britain.

The esoteric tradition in Russia

Organized forms of philosophical and mystical teaching are not just Western imports, however, since they have been a part of Russian culture for many centuries. Esoteric and semi-esoteric orders have also found Russian soil fertile; the order of the Knights of St John of Jerusalem, (otherwise known as the Knights of Malta), with its high-powered rituals, was established in Russia during the reign of Peter the Great, and flourished there officially for a hundred years or so. A branch of the Theosophical Society was founded in Russia in 1908 to promote the teachings of Madame Helena Blavatsky, though it soon had to go underground after it was suppressed following the Bolshevik revolution of 1917. According to today's Russian Theosophical Society, the breakdown of Communism triggered the Society's 'second official birth', although, in fact, its work never really stopped. 'In all these years illegally it led a closed, but spiritually rich life devoted to its ideals'.[1] Other movements too, such as the sacred cosmology and dances taught by Gurdjieff, and the philosophy of his pupil Ouspensky, gained a firm following in Russia before the Revolution, and are said to have continued in secret during all the decades of Communism. And due to the Russian love of the magical and mystical, certain ways of knowledge such as astrology and even perhaps the Kabbala were tolerated to some extent by the authorities; I have heard that some officials and Party members were rather keen on such practices themselves.

The new Christianity

So what we are seeing now is, to some extent, a re-emergence of hidden teachings, as well as an influx of new movements. Although Christianity was of course the official religion in Russia for centuries, it too was severely restricted in Communist times, and is only now returning to full flowering. This means that Russia is still a country of two faiths, the *dvoeverie,* and the Orthodox Church and its twin pole, the indigenous folk tradition, are both alive and well at the present time. As far as the Church is concerned, going to services and having babies baptized is becoming the norm again, rather than the activities of a persecuted minority. Although the Soviet regime paid lip service to freedom of worship, in actual fact most churches were shut down, and turned into warehouses or left to become derelict. Some of my Russian friends have told me how they were baptized in secret by their grandmothers, but could never speak of it openly, otherwise they would not have been promoted at work, and would certainly have been refused permission to travel abroad. Others, who practised their faith overtly, revealed that they were sometimes jostled and taunted on their way into church, and their names were noted by informants, to be used against them later.

One of the unexpected bonuses of this former religious clampdown is the fresh and eager attention with which today's Russians now read the Bible, formerly a text hard to get hold of. 'Then Moses went up the mountain — and do you know what happened next?' one man asked me, keen to share his discoveries. 'Well, yes, I do,' I replied, having survived a marathon of daily Bible readings at school. But what I took for granted and indeed valued in my own culture, was something extraordinary to this person, to whom it was all new. I envied the impact that these stories and teachings were making upon him.

Folk tradition and conscious invention

But it is the body of unwritten traditions and teachings, handed down through the generations, that have been distilled over the centuries, becoming part of the essence of Russia itself, and shaping the Russian soul. So what effect might a new influx of spiritual teachings from the West have upon these, or even a more self-conscious revival of paganism and folk wisdom in Russia? It would be naïve to imagine that there was a Golden Age of the native tradition, when it flowed tranquilly from century to century, untouched by external influences or cultural intervention. Artists, writers, mystics and thinkers have frequently chosen to develop Russian mythology and lore.

One of the first of a new wave of painters in the nineteenth century, keen to portray Russian fairy stories and epic tales, was V.M. Vasnetsov (1848–1926), whom we met briefly in Chapter 1. His pictures have become key images in Russian culture, depicting tender portrayals of folk heroines and heroic and colourful scenes of knights and bards of old. At a humbler level of society, the publishers of the *lubok,* the popular woodcuts sold cheaply on the street and at fairs, also used themes from folklore and magic.

In general, we could say that the body of Russian traditional lore has been both preserved and renewed at all levels of society; as written earlier, the nobility of Czarist Russia also dabbled in magical pursuits and employed healers and diviners. The perpetuation of the Russian tradition does receive conscious input and interpretation, but this does not make it 'artificial', and the continual state of change and exchange has probably helped to enliven and enrich it.

Current interest in Russia in searching the native tradition for magical wisdom is active and growing, as thoughtful Russians measure their own experience gained through meditation, New Age teachings and psychological training, against what their own heritage has to teach them. Sometimes they find teachers among the Russian artists and writers themselves, who are seen as intermediaries between individual creativity and illumination, and the inherited world of folk tradition. One such example is Nicholas Roerich, born in 1874. Roerich was a notable painter, who created scenes not only from his Russian ancestry and the mythology of its deep past, but also from his travels in the Himalayas, and his encounters with Buddhism. Known only in the West as an artist, in Russia he is also revered as a philosopher, who searched for the common truths underlying both Slavic and Asian traditions, who endeavoured to understand human spiritual evolution, and who is credited with the phrase, 'Beauty will save the world,' a toast still popular today with artists lifting their glasses. He has a strong following in Russia, and a museum in Moscow dedicated to him by his admirers.

Pavel Bazhov is another revered figure, a writer living from 1879–1950, who collected folktales in the Ural Mountains and created his own stories from them. These have become household names in Russia, with stories such as *Silver Hoof* and *The Mistress of the Copper Mountain* being especial favourites. But today's Bazhov movement declares that these stories contain hidden esoteric teaching, and his followers have established an organization known as the Bazhov Academy of Secret Knowledge, devoted to extracting the underlying messages from his work (see Chapter 4, note 1). Perhaps this is not as strange as it might at first seem, since stories have always been considered excellent vehicles for carrying knowledge, and the power of Bazhov's imagery, drawn from tradition but enhanced by his own vision, is vivid and haunting.

Other Russian seekers are making their own vision quests and journeys of exploration. A thoughtful account posted on the internet by Larissa Vilenskaya, tempered by both academic knowledge and experience of living in the West, reveals how she progressed from studying traditional Russian teachings about nature spirits, to participating in a group that evokes these spirits, performing its own rituals which involve the eating of a particular type of mushroom. As she writes:

> I came to be in touch with a group of spiritual seekers in Moscow who re-discovered (or, to be more exact, largely re-created by following their inner guidance) ancient sacred mushroom initiation ceremonies. They believe that, during the ceremonies, the spirit of the mushroom guides the participants to healing, facilitates restoring inner harmony, and even, at times, enables them to see the future. One night, I was fortunate enough to be invited to observe such a ceremony in the woods of the Moscow suburbs. Later, I was told that it is not a person but the spirit of the mushroom itself who is believed to choose the participants.

Larissa describes her own revelations and visions, which, although they are obviously stimulated by hallucinogens, are also close to the traditional accounts of nature spirits that have been collected in Russia:

> Everything around me was alive — I was surrounded with tiny gnomes and elves of my childhood fairy tales and could understand the language of trees which granted me healing. Everything was luminous, emanating aura-like light of different colours. From time to time, lightning-like multicoloured flashes appeared, and each splash of a bright colour evoked profound joy, awesome feeling of wonder and reverence.[2]

Facing the future

Over the last twenty years, Russian society has changed dramatically, receiving not only new influences from the West, but also from the thoughts and teachings of its own people, who are now free to write and speak more or less as they like. And the changes are not over yet; more political and economic turbulence is likely before the new Russia finally renews its identity and achieves a stable place on the world stage. It is easy to think that the older Russian culture may be eroded by this impact, but if we were to examine any such transitional period in Russian history in detail, we would probably find there too plenty of cross currents, foreign influences and imaginative development of Russian lore. During the succeeding decades, new input is either absorbed or rejected, and what remains becomes smooth like a stone washed by waters of the river. So this current time of transition and upheaval may, in a hundred years' time, seem like just another turbulent episode in Russia's dramatic history, propelling the nation forward into a new phase, but one in which Russian identity is still clearly discernible.

Change does take place, therefore, but there is still continuity. Amidst all the changes, something remains firmly in place that we can call the Russian tradition, and I have faith that this will be perpetuated into the next generation and beyond. In this book, I have endeavoured to show that it is not the quaint stuff of bygone custom, but rather a living tradition, speaking of the poignant yearnings of the Russian soul, and springing from a uniquely beautiful landscape. To be Russian is to inherit this magical world, and to enter it as a non-Russian is to experience something of its enchantment, and its deep connection with the elements and forces of nature. I hope that my book will provide one such gateway into this world.

Endnotes

Chapter 1

1. This is one of the formulaic traditional phrases used to set a folk or fairy tale in a magical time. See Haney 1999, p.5, and see also Chapter 4 for the belief that humans can understand the language of the birds, pp.99–100.

2. See description, for instance, at http://en.wikipedia.org/wiki/Zbruch_idol.

3. Binary oppositions were proposed by V.V. Ivanov and V.N. Toporov in their attempted reconstruction of the fundamental Slavic cosmology (see Haney 1999, p.48). They are not a new concept, having been proposed in the middle of the twentieth century by the anthropologist Claude Levi-Strauss, who himself based his premise on the philosophy of Hegel. Hegel suggested that every situation contains opposing ideas as 'thesis and antithesis', which are then resolved by 'synthesis'. Levi-Strauss took this concept into anthropology, where he postulated that such binary opposites underlie every society in one form or another; his most famous type of binary pair being 'the raw and the cooked'.

4. As recounted in conversation with cranial-osteopath Peter Cockhill, head of Stillpoint Practice, Bath, UK.

5. Local archaeologists are convinced that life in that area of Khakassia has been preserved to a remarkable degree, and so they use present-day traditions to interpret prehistoric culture: an elk, for instance, is the animal which is said today to carry the departed soul to the underworld, so a pictogram of an elk dating back over 2000 years is usually interpreted in this way.

6. The theme of shamanism and its practices will be explored further at various points in this book, but in order to focus on the Russian tradition itself, it will not be possible to go into full detail and explanation. The Bibliography gives a selection of works on shamanism for further reading.

7. In fact, as Milner-Gulland points out, the migration of the Vikings or Varangians is a complex affair; it is disputed by some authorities, and other influences from Swedes, Greeks, and Iranians, to name but a few, certainly found their way into Russia (Milner-Gulland 1997, pp.36–57).

8. For further reading on the Kabbalistic Tree of Life, see Gilchrist, Cherry and Zur, Gila, *The Tree of Life Oracle* (UK: Connections, USA: Barnes & Noble, 2002).

9. See discussion of the Russian historical and geographical terrain in the Introduction.

10. Milner-Gulland 1997, p.93, quoting from the Primary Chronicle, the key surviving document for earliest records of Russia, composed at about the end of the eleventh century.

11. Haney 1999 has an example of an amusing modern myth told about Lenin, in which a diligent woman worker sewed one of her own buttons onto the great man's jacket when she noticed during his visit to her factory that one of his buttons was missing. She later saw that a portrait of Lenin had been painted showing her button still on his jacket!

12. The *gusli* is one of the earliest known instruments in Russia. The term simply means 'stringed instrument', but it is a kind of harp, which could be held upright, although in the form most usually seen today it is set flat on the knees, more like a psaltery or a dulcimer. For visual examples and descriptions of the *gusli,* see web pages such as: http://en.wikipedia.org/wiki/Gusli, http://www.infoweb.co.nz/gusli, or http://balalajka.dk/english/guslihist.html.

Chapter 2

1. Hubbs 1988, p.26. A complete study of the Goddess Embroideries of Eastern Europe has also been made by Mary B. Kelly (USA: Studio Books, 1989).

2. Classic studies of the goddess are Neumann, Erich, *The Great Mother: Analysis of the Archetype* (Princeton, USA: Princeton University Press, 1955) and Baring, Anne & Cashford, Jules, *The Myth of the Goddess* (London: Viking 1991.) These are valuable source books, and the Baring & Cashford study is particularly well documented and argued. Nevertheless, it does seem that the re-awakening to the existence of 'the goddess' over the last fifty years or so has led to a particular view of her as an amorphous and all-inclusive figure.

3. Further details about St Paraskeva-Friday can be found in Ivanits 1992, pp.33–35.

4. The correct name for Russian nesting dolls is Matrioshka, not Babushka, meaning 'Grandmother', as is sometimes used by Europeans or Americans.

5. See Hubbs 1988, p.xii, although there is little general reinforcement for the Jumala theory; Jumala is more often referred to as a Finnish sky god, the name becoming a word for 'God' in general.

6. See for instance Ivanits 1992, p.15, or http://en.wikipedia.org/wiki/Mokosh.

7. Gilchrist, Cherry, *Following the Firebird* (2007: awaiting publication).

8. For views on the dating of the *bylinis,* see Bailey & Ivanova 1999, p.xvii & pp.3–5.

9. See especially the studies by Hubbs (1988) and Johns (1998), in the Bibliography.

Chapter 3

1. I made the mistake of taking some of these dough balls away with me as a souvenir after such a ritual; I stowed them in my bag and hung them on the head of my bed in the felt yurt tent that we were staying in. Unfortunately, they attracted the attention of a hungry mouse that munched away at them all night! Another member of the travel group said, perhaps jokingly, or perhaps in earnest, that this mouse was the spirit of a rival shaman, come to steal away our shaman's power.

2. This does not include the huge, brick-built country houses now being built in Russia by the newly-rich, who, ironically, use the term 'cottage' (pronounced *kottij* in Russian) to describe their homes.

3. A *dacha* is a term for a weekend cottage, or second home in the country. *Dachas* are owned by a wide cross-section of the population, and may have been built cheek-by-jowl with each other on a parcel of land, and distributed among the workers of a particular factory, for instance. Or they may be individual dwellings, usually smaller than regular village houses, and sometimes ingeniously made of recycled materials such as wooden crates, railway sleepers, and so on. *Dachas* can also be inherited from or shared with relatives. The *dacha* includes a plot of land, and this is the key element, since city folk visit their *dachas* less for a rest than to cultivate fruit and vegetables, which form a vital part of their supplies. If they have no car, they may trek for hours by train or bus to get there, and must do so regularly if the garden is to be kept productive. The *dacha* is still an intrinsic part of Russian culture, even in these changing and more affluent times.

4. The ground floor of Russian houses is often raised by about a meter, so as to allow air to circulate through the foundations, meaning that a cellar may be only partly dug out of the ground.

5. There are parallels here too with the symbolism of alchemy, in which the progression towards the perfection of metallic gold is seen as ascending through the lesser metals, and stages of copper and silver in the alchemical process may be defined as steps towards the final transformation into gold. See Gilchrist, *Explore Alchemy,* Chapter 2, and also p.31: 'The priest, this man of copper, whom you will see seated in the spring, mustering his colour, should not be thought of as a man of

copper, for he has changed the colour of his nature and become a man of silver. If you wish, you will soon have him as a man of gold.' (From Zosimos, *On Virtue,* 4c. ad.)

6. See Kosarev 1999 for an illuminating account of the complexities of shamanic cosmology, and its links to the Slavic traditions.

7. Various folk narratives of experiences with *domavoi* can be found in Ivanits 1992, pp.169–77.

8. Milner-Gulland 1997, p.32, quoting an account supposedly reported by St Andrew to the Romans, and included in the Primary Chronicle, the key surviving historical record of Russia.

9. Fire and water are commonly said to be warring elements in magical schema, such as that of alchemy, where the goal of transformation is sometimes described as the union of fire and water: in other words, the successful integration of conflicting opposites.

10. A comprehensive list of popular divination methods can be found in Ryan 1999, Chapter 4.

11. See Milner-Gulland 1997, p.33, where he also quotes the source of this idea, *Binary Models in the Dynamics of Russian Culture,* the work of the influential writers Yu. Lotman and B. Uspensky. This description of the polarity between the Red Corner and the bathhouse has been picked up by other writers in the field too, and is certainly a useful model to clarify the spiritual layout of the home and the cosmology that it embodies.

12. See Worobec 1991, pp.159–74, for a full description of the traditional wedding ceremony.

13. This particular version of a common divination game comes from informants on Kiji Island, in the far north.

14. For a full description and history of lacquer miniatures, see Gilchrist, Cherry (1999) *Russian Lacquer Miniatures.*

15. A superb analysis of Russian music and its relationship to Russian folk roots was given in a series of television programmes broadcast on BBC 4, called *All the Russias,* and presented by Valeri Gergiev, director of the Marinsky theatre orchestra.

16. The Izmailovo craft market is situated towards the edge of the city, and is well known for its array of crafts, paintings, and antiques. Over the last few years, it has been brushing up its image for visitors, and new wooden buildings have been commissioned there which are decorated in the style of Russian fairy tales.

Chapter 4

1. This story is told by Pavel Bazhov (1879–1950), who collected similar stories from miners in the Urals who extracted precious stones from the mountains; his *Tales from the Ural Mountains* are based on these, and contain various themes of gemstones. The collection has become famous throughout Russia, especially stories such as *Silver Hoof,* and *The Mistress of the Copper Mountain,* which are often printed and translated separately.

2. See, for example, the words of *The Queen's Epicedium: Elegy on the death of Queen Mary, 1695,* set to music by the English composer Henry Purcell, which concludes: 'Stella sua fixa/ Coelum ultra lucet,' or 'Her star, immovable, shines on in the heavens.'

3. The idea of time, and of the cycles that it embodies, combining with the sense of foreknowledge and the creation of calendar rituals, will be explored further in the final chapter.

4. For an account of early astrology, see Michael Baigent's *From the Omens of Babylon: Astrology and Ancient Mesopotamia* (London: Penguin Arkana, 1994).

5. See http://www.bibletime.com/new/log/2004/09/18/Putin/.

6. Warner, E. (2002) 'Death by Lightning: For Sinner or Saint? Beliefs from Novoskol'niki Region, Pskov Province, Russia' in *Topics, Notes and Comments,* The Folklore Society.

7. See the example given of Khokhloma lacquered ware in Chapter 3, p.75.

8. The classical symbol of the Caduceus, traditionally associated with Hermes, the wise guide and trickster spirit, is a useful example of this. It consists of a straight staff with two serpents twining around it, and can be seen as the straight line of intention, which is only completed by the winding paths formed by the serpents; we cannot go directly to the goal, and our will must be pliable, yielding to the conditions we meet, and moving around the obstacles in our path.

9. White, Antonia (1954), *Beyond the Glass,* republished 1979 by Virago Press, London, pp.214–6.

10. For more details of the author's experience of a consultation with the shaman, see 'The Russian Spirit of Place', Chapter 7 in *Sky and Psyche* (2006).

11. The story of *The Bluebird of Happiness* was written as a modern fairy tale by Maurice Maeterlink in the early twentieth century, and turned into a film starring Shirley Temple in 1940; it was, incidentally, produced

as a remake in 1976 in a joint USA/Soviet production! The symbol of the bluebird as a sacred bird and a herald of happiness seems to be significant in American and Native American Indian culture too, and other instances of it occur in different traditions around the world.

12. See David Abram's *The Spell of the Sensuous* for a general investigation of the animate worldview, which the author contends is less archaic and out of reach than generally believed.

Chapter 5

1. This piece, entitled 'The Hut on Hen's Legs', was inspired by a drawing of Baba Yaga's house, made by Viktor Hartmann.

2. See papers by Dianne E. Farrell (1993) and Andreas Johns (1998) cited in the Bibliography, and references in Haney 1999.

3. See Gilchrist, Cherry (1988) *The Circle of Nine.* The Nine Muses of classical myth are also said to be descended from three original goddesses.

4. Marian Bowman contends that there is no such thing as an entirely orthodox set of individual beliefs, in terms of official religion: 'I would like to suggest that accounts of religion which do not take into account folk religion risk telling less than the whole story. . . . At the individual level, religion is a mixture of a received religious tradition and a personal belief system.' (Bowman, Marian, 'Phenomenology, Fieldwork and Folk Religion', in *British Association for the Study of Religions,* Occasional Papers, no.6, 1992.) It has also been shown that a large percentage of Americans (27%) believe in reincarnation, although it is not a part of the official set of beliefs. (See Harris Poll, 2003, at www.harrisinteractive.com.) Reincarnation, of course, is a perfectly respectable doctrine in Buddhism and Hinduism, although that seems to be overlooked when popular media has derided Prince Charles for his interest in such 'loony' subjects. Reincarnation does seem to be a naturally occurring belief. My own father, who was strict in his Christian views, once admitted to me that as a boy he had been convinced that he was an Egyptian priest in a past life.

5. See article posted on Friendship Roads Travel Company, at http://www.ddfr.ru.

6. Perhaps the Christian belief in the devil is at work here, attributing a devil's tail to the fledgling sorcerer.

7. For studies of an animate or conscious universe, based on sound academic research, but which are thoroughly accessible to the lay reader, see for instance Abram, David, *The Spell of the Sensuous,* Fontana, David, *Is there an Afterlife?* also Sheldrake, Rupert *The Sense of Being Stared At,* and Campion, N. & Curry, P (eds.) *Sky and Psyche.*

8. For an overall survey of divination methods, see Gilchrist: *Divination*. For an analysis of the many divination methods used in the Russian tradition, see Ryan 1999, Chapters 4 & 5.

9. See Haney 1999, pp.65–71, for an excellent review of the bear cult in Russia.

10. The duck is often associated with creation myths, both in the Finnish tradition (which links to ancient Slavic mythology) and in Siberian legends. A tale is told in the Khakassia province of Siberia about two ducks, which created the earth between them. First of all, the world was nothing but emptiness, but then the emptiness became filled with water, and two ducks appeared sitting on it. Tired of just floating, they decided to make land and mountains by diving for silt to shape them with. One of the ducks stole two of the stones, which angered her sister as it disturbed the pattern they were making, and she was subsequently dismissed to become ruler of the underworld, while the righteous duck remained queen of the upper regions.

Chapter 6

1. Russians often use the word 'rest' in English to mean relaxation, or taking a break, as this is the simplest way to translate the verb *otdixat'*.

2. 'The Kind Woodcutter', in Zheleznova, *Tales of the Amber Sea*. This story is from the Baltic regions, which are now independent of Russia, but which share a broadly similar folk heritage.

3. Adapted from 'Ivan Tsarevich and the Gray Wolf', in Haney 2001, vol.I, p.199.

4. For more about Koshchei the Deathless, see Chapter 5, p.128f.

5. See Ivanits 1992, pp.75–81, for a discussion of the different characteristics of the *rusalka* and her ambivalence in the realm of folklore.

Chapter 7

1. The Gregorian calendar was introduced into various countries over the course of several centuries, to correspond more accurately with the movement of the sun, and to correct the inaccuracies that had slipped in and taken the year somewhat out of kilter. Its adoption in Britain provoked riots in 1752, when people believed that they were losing eleven days out of their lives, as the calendar was made to jump eleven days forwards.

2. *Khorovod:* a traditional circle dance (see also Fig. 23).

3. See Gilchrist, *Alchemy*, pp.20–24 and 55–60, including, too, a discus-

sion on the alchemical nature of dew.

4. http://www.uoregon.edu/~kimball/tarkovsky.rublev.htm#21.

Epilogue

1. See http://www.theosophy.ru/ehistory.htm.

2. See 'From Slavic Mysteries to Contemporary Psi Research and Back' at http://resonateview.org/places/writings/larissa/myth.htm.

Bibliography

Russian Life and History

Gerhart, Genevra (1994) *The Russian's World,* Holt, Rhinehart & Winston, USA.

Fraser, Eugenie (1984) *The House by the Dvina: A Russian Childhood* (Corgi, UK).

Hubbs, Joanna (1988) *Mother Russia,* Indiana University Press, Bloomington & Indianapolis.

Milner-Gulland, R. (1997) *The Russians,* Blackwell, USA.

Van der Post, Laurens (1965) *Journey into Russia,* Penguin Books, London.

Worobec, Christine D. (1991) *Peasant Russia: Family and Community in the Post-Emancipation Period,* Princeton University Press, New Jersey.

Russian traditional art and culture

Billington, James H. (1970) *The Icon and the Axe,* Vintage Books: Random House, New York.

Gaynor, Elizabeth, Haavisto, Kari & Goldstein, Darra (no date) *Russian Houses,* Benedikt Taschen Verlag, Cologne, Germany.

Gilchrist, Cherry (1999) *Russian Lacquer Miniatures,* Firebird Publications, Bristol.

—, (2006) 'The Russian Spirit of Place', in *Sky and Psyche,* eds. Campion, N. and Curry, P., Floris Books, Edinburgh.

Haney, Jack V. (1999) *An Introduction to the Russian Folktale,* M.E. Sharpe, Armonk, New York & England.

Hilton, Alison (1995) *Russian Folk Art,* Indiana University Press, Bloomington and Indianapolis.

Hubbs, Joanna (1988) *Mother Russia: The Feminine Myth in Russian Culture,* Indiana University Press, Bloomington and Indianapolis.

Ivanits, Linda J. (1992) *Russian Folk Belief,* M.E. Sharpe, Armonk, New York & England.

Kourenoff, Paul M., & St George, George (1970) *Russian Folk Medicine,* W.H. Allen, London & New York.

Krasunov, V.K. (ed.) (1996) *Russian Traditions,* Kitizdat, Nizhni Novgorod.

Phillips, C. & Kerrigan, M. (1999) *Forests of the Vampire,* Time-Life Books, with Duncan Baird Publishers, Amsterdam and London.

Reeder, Roberta (1975) *Russian Folk Lyrics,* University of Pennsylvania Press, USA.

Rozhnova, P. (1992) *A Russian Folk Calendar,* Novosti, Moscow.

Ryan, W.F. (1999) *The Bathhouse at Midnight: Magic in Russia,* Sutton Publishing Ltd., Stroud, UK.

Soloviova, L.N. (1997) *Matryoshka,* Interbook, Moscow.

Weiss, Peg (1995) *Kandinsky and Old Russia,* Yale University Press, New Haven & London.

Zenkovsky, S.A. (ed.) (1963) *Medieval Russia's Epics, Chronicles and Tales,* Meridian, New York.

Russian Legends, Folk & Fairy Tales

Afanasiev, Aleksandr (1973) *Russian Fairy Tales,* trans. Norbert Guterman, Random House, New York.

—, (1978) *The Magic Ring,* Raduga Publishers, Moscow.

—, (1981) *The Three Kingdoms,* Raduga Publishers, Moscow.

—, (1983), *Words of Wisdom,* Raduga Publishers, Moscow.

Bailey, James & Ivanova, Tatyana (1999) *An Anthology of Russian Folk Epics,* M.E. Sharpe, New York.

Gilchrist, Cherry (1994) *Prince Ivan and the Firebird,* Barefoot Books, Bristol.

Haney, Jack V. (2001) *Russian Wondertales* (two vols), M.E. Sharpe, New York. Maxym, Lucy (1986) *Russian Lacquer Legends vol II,* Siamese Imports Co., Hisksville, NY.

New Larousse Encyclopedia of Mythology (1969), Paul Hamlyn Group, London.

Riordan, James (1989) *The Sun Maiden and the Crescent Moon — Siberian Folktales,* Interlink Books, New York.

Warner, E. (1985) *Heroes, Monsters and Other Worlds from Russian Mythology,* Eurobook, UK.

Zheleznova, Irina (1987) (ed.) *Tales of the Amber Sea,* Raduga Press, Moscow.

Shamanism

Diószegi V. and Hoppál M. (1978) *Shamanism in Siberia,* Akadémiai Kiadó, Budapest.

Drury, Nevill (1989) *The Elements of Shamanism,* Element Books, Shaftesbury, UK.

Eliade, Mircea (1964) *Shamanism: Archaic Techniques of Ecstasy,* in 1989 edition, Penguin Arkana, London.

Gorbatcheva, V. and Federova, M. (2000) *The Peoples of the Great North: Art and Civilization of Siberia,* Parkstone Press, New York.

Harvey, G. (2003) *Shamanism, A Reader,* Routledge, London & New York.

Hutton, Ronald (2001) *Shamans: Siberian Spirituality and the Western Imagination,* Hambledon & London, London and New York.

'Sarangarel' (Julie Ann Stewart) (2000) *Riding Windhorses,* Destiny Books, Vermont.

Stutley, M. (2003) *Shamanism: An Introduction,* Routledge, London.

Vitebsky, P. (1995) *The Shaman: Voyages of the Soul,* Duncan Baird, London.

General

Abram, David (1997) *The Spell of the Sensuous,* Vintage Books, New York.

Campion, N. & Curry, P., eds. (2006) *Sky and Psyche,* Floris Books, Edinburgh.

Fontana, David (2005) *Is there an Afterlife? A Comprehensive Overview of the Evidence,* O Books, UK.

Gilchrist, Cherry, (1987) *Divination: The Search for Meaning,* Dryad Press, London.

—, (1988) *The Circle of Nine: The feminine psyche revealed through nine contemporary archetypes,* Penguin Arkana, London.

—, (2002) *Everyday Alchemy,* Rider, London.

—, (2007) *Explore Alchemy,* (formerly *The Elements of Alchemy*), Heart of Albion Press, Loughborough, UK.

Paine, Sheila (1994) *The Afghan Amulet,* Penguin, London.

—, (1998) *The Golden Horde,* Penguin, London.

Sheldrake, Rupert (2003) *The Sense of Being Stared At, and other Aspects of the Extended Mind*, Arrow, UK.

Papers

Farrell, Dianne E., (1993) 'Shamanic Elements in Some Early Eighteenth Century Russian Woodcuts' in *Slavic Review*, vol.52:4, pp.725–44.

Johns, Andreas (1998) 'Baba Iaga and the Russian Mother' in *The Slavic and East European Journal*, vol. 42, No.1.

Kenin-Lopsan, with Boraxoo, M. & Taylor, E. (1997) 'Tuvinian Shamans and the Cult of Birds', in *ReVision*, vol.19.3, p.33.

Kosarev, M.F. (1999) 'The System of the Universe in Pagan Siberian Indigenous Peoples', in *Astronomical & Astrophysical Transactions*, vol.17: 6.

Journals

Russian Life, www.russian-life.com (Montpelier, VT, USA.)

Other resources

For lacquer miniatures to view and purchase, visit the author's website at: www.firebirdarts.co.uk.

For other books by Cherry Gilchrist, and information about the author, including available talks and lectures, see www.cherrygilchrist.co.uk.

Index

A note on this index:

Since the magical and symbolic content of Russian culture predominates in this book, many of the entries in the index refer to passages describing this aspect of the theme in question rather than to passing mentions or mundane use of a word. But despite the importance of the magical world view here, the word 'magic' itself is too general to find a significant place in the index; searching under more specific headings like 'divination,' 'ritual', and 'nature spirits' will give more fruitful results.

Quest Books
encourages open-minded inquiry into
world religions, philosophy, science, and the arts
in order to understand the wisdom of the ages,
respect the unity of all life, and help people explore
individual spiritual self-transformation.

Its publications are generously supported by
The Kern Foundation,
a trust committed to Theosophical education.

Quest Books is the imprint of
the Theosophical Publishing House,
a division of the Theosophical Society in America.
For information about programs, literature,
on-line study, membership benefits, and international centers,
see www.theosophical.org
or call 800-669-1571 or (outside the U.S.) 630-668-1571.

Related Quest Titles

Celebrate the Solstice, by Richard Heinberg

The Dove in the Stone, by Alice O. Howell

Earth Energies, by Serge King

The Quest for the Green Man, by John Matthews

The Real St. Nicholas, by Louise Carus

The Real World of Fairies, by Dora van Gelder

The Summer Solstice, by John Matthews

The Winter Solstice, by John Matthews

To order books or a complete Quest catalog,
call 800-669-9425 or (outside the U.S.) 630-665-0130.

Cherry Gilchrist is a long-time participant in Western traditions relating to the Kabbala, hermeticism, and meditation. A graduate of Cambridge University, UK, in English and Anthropology, she holds a postgraduate diploma from the University of Bath Spa in Cultural Astronomy and Astrology. Her focus is on finding hidden or lost wisdom in ancient and oral traditions and exploring the bridge between the esoteric and exoteric worlds.

Having published widely, Cherry writes both for adults and for children and has won a UK Reading Award for her book *A Calendar of Festivals.* Her other books include *The Alchemist's Path, Stories from the Silk Road, The Circle of Nine,* and *Divination.* Many of her titles have been translated into other languages, including Italian, French, German, Spanish and Portuguese.

With something of the merchant also in her blood, Cherry has made nearly sixty trips to Russia in search of beautiful lacquer miniatures and the rich heritage of Russian folklore and crafts. She ran a Russian arts gallery in Bath, England, for a number of years and has produced leading exhibitions of Russian folk art at museums and galleries. She is also a well-known lecturer on Russian art and culture and inner traditions. For more information visit www.cherrygilchrist.co.uk.

Praise for Cherry Gilchrist's

Russian Magic

"I highly recommend this marvelous book. The author reminds us of what too many have forgotten: that at the heart of human cultures is living nature, as manifest in local animals, places, and the land."

Patrick Curry, Ph.D., Lecturer in Religious Studies at the University of Kent

"Cherry Gilchrist reveals an extraordinary open-mindedness regarding the continued practice of ancient rituals and customs, a landscape empowered with unusual forces and a supernatural world inhabited by spirits, pagan gods, shamans, wizards, witches, and psychic healers. Highly recommended."

The Cauldron, May 2008

"Cherry Gilchrist has been visiting Russia for sixteen years and has caught something of the national character. She has walked home on a warm summer's evening, hearing folk songs in the distance and seeing bonfires glow against the twilight. She mingles with the crowd at the carnival of Maslnitsa and lived for a while in a traditional log-built home. She even has her own house spirit or domavoi. . . . She turns to folktales for the deep wisdom they contain and unearths the magic buried in everyday Russian life."

Fortean Times, July 2008

"The author takes us on a spiritually rich tour . . . and demonstrates that the idea of the 'soul' plays a central part in the Russian mindset. . . . Exploring the spiritual traditions of Russia, the book is complete with tales of magic and witchcraft and examines how this affects the psyche of the people who live there today."

Soul and Spirit, August 2008

The first time any Westerner has understood the Russian soul.

—**Alexander Prior,** Musician and Composer

The Firebird, Snowmaiden, Father Frost, Baba Yaga . . . the names of such beloved Russian fairy-tale characters evoke a magical world. Yet Russia's rich folk culture is usually seen only as a backdrop to political and historical studies. For the first time, Cherry Gilchrist shows how Russian fairy tales, native wisdom, and folk art are interrelated. The Russian people—archaeologists, scientists, doctors, and country folk alike—feel a close bond with their vast and scenic landscape and share a keen interest in psychic phenomena and faith healing. Gilchrist mines their awareness and brings an animated universe to life with

- Animal tales, myths, and legends
- Eyewitness accounts of magical creatures
- Rituals, charms, beliefs, and prophesies
- Herbalism and healing
- The magical worldview's influence on art and architecture

With gorgeous illustrations, here is probably the best guide to Russian lore available in English today. Entering its fascinating realm can lead us into the soul of our own landscape and inspire us to magical creativity in our own lives.

"For all lovers of Story and the Russia of endless steppes and forests of dream, this book weaves a song of hope for the soul of 'moist Mother Earth' and all who dwell upon Her. Great pictures, too."

—***Inner Light Magazine***

Cherry Gilchrist is the author of many books on mythology, traditional culture, and inner traditions, including *The Alchemist's Path, Stories from the Silk Road, A Calendar of Festivals, The Circle of Nine,* and *Divination.*

U.S. $18.95 / CAN. $21.50

Folklore / Metaphysics

www.questbooks.net